Contents:

Lure of the
CARIBBEAN
Virgin Islands to Trinidad

Created by Ted Czolowski

Text by Donald Stainsby

A Quest
Travelbook

RAND McNALLY & COMPANY
Chicago   New York   San Francisco

Introduction

The West Indies lie scattered on the surface of the Caribbean Sea like so many stepping stones, forming a path that led white men ashore on the mainland of the American continents. They curl gracefully eastward and south from the Gulf of Mexico to the north coast of South America, a great arc of beauty, of sunshine, of history, of legend and romance.

In our customary arrogance, ignoring the civilizations that were before us, we say it was Columbus who saw them first. Soon the explorer's cockleshells were followed by whole armadas of galleons bringing soldiers and black-robed priests, settlers and looters who stripped the lands of their treasure and sent it home to Spain. The treasure in turn brought pirates, privateers and freebooters, and that peculiarly Caribbean breed, the buccaneer, which preyed only on Spanish ships sailing upon the Spanish Main.

These islands have trembled under the advancing feet of the *conquistadors* and they have cowered beneath the guns of Hawkins and Drake. They have suffered the backlash of European wars. They have witnessed the extermination of a race, and they saw the first Africans to be brought to the brave new world in slavery.

Today the tempests have in the main subsided. Many of the islands struggle to make their independence work, and the hordes descending upon them now come by jet to laze on the beaches, to fish, to enjoy the sprightly sounds of steel bands or run their hands along the weathered stone walls while contemplating the fabled past. For the visitor, these islands in the sun are themselves a treasure trove.

Columbus thought he had made his landfall off the coast of Asia, so he called them the West Indies. Others thought he had stumbled upon the lost continent of Atlantis, the storied Antillia, so they called them the Antilles. The larger islands lay in the main to the north and became the Greater Antilles, a continuation of the mountain range that forms the backbone of Mexico and Central America. The smaller islands were grouped along the outer eastern edge and came to be known as the Lesser Antilles. It is these islands, lesser in size only, that we deal with here.

From the Virgin Islands the Lesser Antilles stretch about 700 miles south and southeast to Trinidad, which once was joined to the South American Caribbean coastal range. The other islands in the Lesser Antilles group are of two types. To the north an outer arc of low islands stretches from Anguilla to Marie Galante; these are old volcanoes, planed down by the sea, at one time having been submerged and covered by marine sediments, including limestone. Most of the group lies in the inner arc, stretching from Saba to Grenada. These, too, are volcanic islands, younger and therefore higher and, in some cases, still slightly active.

The Lesser Antilles lie between 10 and 18 degrees north latitude, where the high angle of the near-equatorial sun gives them a sea-level temperature averaging about 80°F during the warm months and around 75°F during the cooler season.

It was the trade winds that first brought the white men to the Lesser Antilles. Although sailors had known for centuries how to determine latitude, they could not calculate longitude. So when Columbus and those who followed him wished to get to the West Indies they merely sailed south until they picked up the trades, turned their bows to the west and let the winds do the rest. This method of navigation, effective though it was, has led to some confusion in the matter of designating the islands.

For when the Spanish entered the West Indies, they landed first in the Lesser Antilles. The Greater Antilles were therefore downwind and so became known as the Leeward Islands. The Lesser Antilles became known as the Windward Islands, because most of them lay to windward, or upwind, of the Spanish landfall. This made sense so long as Spain was alone in the Caribbean.

But unfortunately, Spain wasn't alone long. When ships of other nations entered the region, they usually tried to make a landfall at the high island of Dominica. Through the years the Lesser Antilles north of

Dominica became known as the Leeward Islands, probably because they were on the leeward *side* of Dominica even though some were often upwind. The islands south of Dominica remained known as the Windward Islands.

The trade winds were Columbus' first important discovery when he left the Canary Islands, and they carried him to the Bahamas in just 36 days. He continued west to Cuba, then doubled back to Hispaniola, occupied today by Haiti and the Dominican Republic.

On these islands he met the Arawaks, an easy going, friendly people who made two contributions to western culture—the hammock, and the practice of inhaling the smoke of burning tobacco leaves. The Arawaks wore nose-plugs, necklaces and bracelets of gold, which they traded to the Spaniards—and sealed their own doom. For these baubles helped spur further Spanish exploration and settlement, and within twenty years the Arawaks had been wiped out.

Columbus made a hero's return to Spain and King Ferdinand was quick to send him back to the new found lands. The king was also quick to get the Pope, the Spaniard Alexander VI, to issue a series of papal bulls which, among other things, declared that all lands west of a line 100 leagues west of the Azores (later 370 leagues west) were to belong to Spain. New lands to the east of this line were to be Portugal's. (In time, these were to include Brazil and the west coast of Africa with its slave stations.)

On his third voyage in 1498, Columbus sailed far enough south to discover Trinidad and the mouth of the Orinoco River before turning north to Hispaniola, which for the next twenty years was the base of exploration and conquest.

The sugar plantations and the gold mines on Hispaniola and Cuba required a great labor force. On his third voyage Columbus established the *repartimiento* system, which divided the native population among the settlers as servants and laborers. More important, it prepared the way, both emotionally and legally, for another system that was to have far-reaching effects.

The *repartimiento* system spread throughout the Spanish colonies, but even it was not enough. The Spaniards sought to impress Lucayos from the Bahamas, but the natives killed themselves rather than submit to forced labor. Then in 1510 the Spanish government authorized the shipment of 250 slaves from Africa to work Hispaniola's gold mines. In 1518, Charles V of Spain granted a trading licence to supply 4,000 African slaves to Hispaniola. The licence in time passed to the Portuguese, who—by virtue of the papal bull granting them West Africa—found themselves with a monopoly on the West Indian slave trade.

Significantly, production in Hispaniola's gold mines increased as the slaves came, reaching its peak in 1518, then declining rapidly. But there were other mines, notably in Cuba. Cuba was less mountainous and more fertile than Hispaniola and so offered better opportunities for ranching, tobacco farming, and sugar planting. In fact, Spain's headquarters moved to Cuba in 1519 when Cortés sailed from Cuba to conquer Mexico. In 1522 Pizarro was in Peru. By 1525 there were Spaniards on the northern coasts of South America, which became known as the Spanish Mainland, or the "Spanish Main", a name that was to become intimately—and romantically—associated with the sea that lay off that coast, a sea laden with treasure ships that inevitably drew the attention of the outside world.

The trade of the Spanish colonies was controlled by monopolies in Cadiz. All cargoes to and from the colonies had to be in Spanish ships, and the colonists were forbidden to trade with any nation but Spain, even though Spain could not fully supply their needs. The colonies' treasure was shipped home twice a year in huge flotillas which gathered in Havana harbor.

These two lures, treasure ships and dissatisfied colonies hungry for trade, attracted various kinds of more or less unsavory entrepreneurs—smugglers, pirates and freebooters, privateers and buccaneers.

Some distinctions must be made. Smugglers are known the world over, merely trading without benefit of tariffs. Pirates are outlawed by all nations, preying on any vessels anywhere. Freebooters were not, precisely, pirates. They used force to acquire, free, the booty of treasure ships. They were financed by businessmen who purchased shares in the venture and when the ships returned declared dividends in a strict businesslike way. Privateers were not pirates either, but operated privately owned ships under licence— "letters of marque"—from their own government against the vessels of some other nation. Buccaneers were strictly a Caribbean innovation.

The word comes from the French *boucanier*, which is borrowed from Brazil and originally meant one who smokes meat over a fire on a *boucan*, a frame something like a barbecue. The name was first applied to French hunters in Santo Domingo, who enlivened their pastoral life with occasional essays in robbing. Eventually one of them, Pierre Le Grande, took after a Spanish ship so successfully that others followed him. They established

their headquarters in Tortuga and eventually the word "buccaneer" came to be applied to all the pirates operating against Spanish ships in the Caribbean Sea, the so-called "Spanish Main".

Oddly enough, it was also the French who started the freebooting business when in 1523 French ships off the Azores seized two vessels carrying treasure from Mexico, including gold, jewels, plumes, and 680 pounds of pearls. Such raids became so successful that in 1543 the Spanish started sending their treasure fleets home in heavily guarded convoys. However, the colonial ports were not adequately defended. In 1554, Francois "Timberleg" le Clerc captured Santiago, and in the following year his lieutenant, Jacques Sores, captured and razed Havana itself.

This sort of thing made the colonists understandably jumpy. As soon as unfamiliar sails were spotted on the horizon, residents of the ports would gather up their valuables and head for the hills. This in turn made things difficult for bona fide smugglers who dropped by solely to do business, which is where the English enter the scene in the person of John Hawkins.

Financed by businessmen in Plymouth, Hawkins sailed in 1562, becoming the first foreigner to violate Portugal's monopoly on slaves by picking up about 400 Africans on his way to the Indies. The colonists, who may not have seen a legitimate supply ship for months or even years, were eager to trade—so eager that Hawkins pursued the business. On his third trip he was accompanied by a cousin, a young man in his 20s named Francis Drake. They were surprised at San Juan de Ulua by portions of a Spanish fleet, lost several of their ships and barely escaped themselves. Red-headed, like his queen, Drake neither forgot nor forgave.

He made more trips and, in 1572, when Spain and England broke off relations, became a privateer, capturing in Panama three treasure-laden mule trains from Peru. He arrived home in triumph; Queen Elizabeth put a knighthood on his shoulders while the Spanish put a price on his head. Drake continued to ravage the Indies, capturing Santo Domingo and Cartagena.

Smugglers, slavers, freebooters, and buccaneers became more bold, setting up their own market places at the northern end of the Lesser Antilles.

So, with something of the rich and romantic legacy of the entire region in our minds, a good place to begin our close look at the islands of the Lesser Antilles is in the Virgin Islands.

VIRGIN ISLANDS

Columbus discovered the Virgin Islands in 1492. Seeing the large number of islands and the way the sea hurled itself upon the rocks, sending up towers of spray that looked like a procession of robed figures, he named them the Islands of the Eleven Thousand Virgins in honor of St. Ursula and her colleagues. Ironically, in the years since, these islands have been the location of the richest free port in the Antilles, the busiest slave market in the Caribbean, the bustling head-quarters of pirates, the lavish production of rum, and a rollicking vacation center. During all that time they have remained the Virgins.

Columbus erred slightly in his count. There are actually only about 100 Virgin Islands, including rocks and cays, with a total land area of about 200 square miles. Over 50 islands, about 130 square miles, are under American control. The remaining 60 or so square miles are made up of more than 40 islands that have been a colony of Great Britain since 1671.

The British islands are the eastern part of the

Virgins. They enclose Sir Francis Drake Channel, sheltered water that many yachtsmen consider to be one of the finest sailing areas in the world. The channel runs northeast from the American islands to Virgin Gorda (Big Virgin). Once mined for its copper, the island today is a growing resort area, prized for its many sheltered bays and beaches.

Off the southeast point of Virgin Gorda, a row of pinnacles called Fallen Jerusalem begins a scattering of small islands that form the southern boundary of Drake Channel. One of these islands is Dead Man's Chest of "Yo-ho-ho" fame. The northern boundary is formed largely by the island of Tortola (Turtle Dove), a former sugar island that is the largest of the British chain, and its capital.

Tortola and Virgin Gorda supply produce, live-stock, and fish for the tables of St. Thomas. Many of the younger people of the British islands work in the American islands, sending money home to their families in the British islands, whose currency, as a result, is American money.

The American islands include the three biggest in the chain: St. Thomas, St. John and, 40 miles south, St. Croix. St. Croix was originally settled by the French, and was bought in 1733 by the Danes, who had previously settled both St. Thomas and St. John. Denmark in turn sold all three to the United States in 1917.

St. Croix, whose name is pronounced San Croy, is not geologically part of the mountain chain of the rest of the Virgins. Flatter than the other islands and, with 84 square miles, the largest, St. Croix was a wealthy sugar island. Sugar died out, was revived, then phased out, but may yet come back. St. Croix is the main producer of Virgin Islands rum, and very good rum it is, too.

Architecture buffs will find much to enjoy in St. Croix's two main towns. Christiansted's buildings are still largely Danish of the 18th century, preserved or restored; Frederiksted was burned down in 1878 and rebuilt of wood in the giddy Gothic of the Victorian period, producing buildings that are a mixture of the rather touching and the frankly hilarious. People who know the islands well say that the social atmosphere of St. Croix is Boston Brahmin, compared to the bustling New York of St. Thomas.

Although its lush, hilly beauty is now almost a primitive wilderness, St. John too was once a sugar plantation island. In 1733 the slaves revolted against their Danish masters, many of whom abandoned their plantations to squatters and nature. Recently Laurance Rockefeller purchased 5,000 acres of St. John and turned it over to the government, which declared it a national park.

Neighboring St. Thomas is a world in itself. Rather, it's two worlds, divided—though not separated—by the mountain spine that runs from east to west.

The south side of the ridge, centered around the harbor of Charlotte Amalie, the capital, contains the public life of St. Thomas. Here are the port facilities, the free port shops, the hotels and restaurants, the government offices, and the town houses of the residents. Here is where life swings for residents and visitors, especially during carnival.

The northern side is where the private life of the island is lived. There are some resort developments out on the eastern end of St. Thomas (top left, with St. John beyond) and the beginnings of residential suburbs on the western end. Along the north side there are private homes and truck gardens on the wooded hills that slope down to enclose beautiful bays and occasional quiet beaches.

Two bays on the eastern end of St. Thomas, with other Virgin Islands lying beyond.

North shore bays, St. Thomas. At the bottom is Magen's Bay, with its mile-long crescent of public beach.

13

Charlotte Amalie from a tramway car. From the top of this hill you can see about 500 square miles of island-studded sea.

Directly below is the yacht harbor. Above it is the city waterfront, where inter-island ships tie up.

The present waterfront is along a filled-in area. The old wharves were alongside warehouses that have been converted and redecorated into shops selling international goods at 40 to 60 per cent below American prices. Charlotte Amalie's status as a free port was written into the treaty by which Denmark sold the Virgin Islands to the United States.

Charlotte Amalie contains more hundred-year-old buildings still in use than any other city in the United States. Several have been officially designated out-standing historical buildings and the Danish government has recorded some of them to show their influence on Danish architecture at home. For many Danes returned home to settle after making their fortunes in sugar and even bigger fortunes in trade.

The Danes kept themselves neutral and their port wide open for over two hundred years. Charlotte Amalie often harbored ships of rival warring nations as well as a steady flow of pirates selling their booty. The tolerant attitude also made St. Thomas a haven for political and religious refugees, and for years the community benefited from the presences of cultured emigrés.

St. Thomas continues to be a haven for escapists of many sorts.

From the waterfront, Charlotte Amalie clambers up three hills, Denmark, Government, and Synagogue. The last one can be climbed on *Raadets Gade*, the street at the left: at the top you'll find the second oldest *synagogue* under the American flag, whose entrance is shown above. Many years ago, its congregation included the parents of Camille Pissaro, one of the founders of Impressionist art. Pissaro was born and raised in Charlotte Amalie, in a home that is over the present site of a Sears store on Main St.

(*Overleaf*) *A Main Street scene and carnival fireworks.*

Carnival, which is so lively in predominantly Catholic islands, did not become a pre-Lenten celebration in Danish Lutheran St. Thomas. Not to be deprived of their fun, St. Thomians held carnival at the beginning of the sugar harvest. Now held during the last week in April, it's an ear-splitter. These pictures were taken during the big wind-up parade.

Carnival is a wild, mixed-up, happy view of the Virgin Islands, which are themselves sometimes mixed up. They are a place where original settlers paid the governor rent of a turkey a year per 125 acres; land now goes as high as $30,000 an acre—and up. They're a place where necessities are expensive and luxuries are cheap—water bills are a constant source of anguish to residents; the best rum in the world costs about a dollar a bottle. The man who designed America's national capital in Washington was born and raised in the British Virgin Islands, and Edward Teach, the pirate Blackbeard, had a home in Charlotte Amalie. Today it's a place where men whose income once ran to five or six figures are happily running shops or small businesses and natives are living comfortably by renting their land to men whose income runs to five or six figures. With its deceptive American veneer, it's a good place to begin to savor the unexpected joys of the Lesser Antilles.

A last look at the Virgin Islands from Synagogue Hill, eastward down Crystal Gade.

LEEWARD ISLANDS

In addition to the Virgin Islands, the Leeward Islands—in the modern, non-Spanish parlance—include Antigua, and Guadeloupe, as well as such smaller islands as St. Kitts and Nevis, Montserrat, and St. Martin. These few named here reflect the chequered history of the whole Lesser Antilles—the push and pull of British, French, and Dutch.

As we have seen, Spain never was strong in the Lesser Antilles, her role being more that of a catalyst to other powers. In the early part of the 17th century, for example, her lowland provinces—the Netherlands—were fighting for their independence. A small country without many natural resources, the Dutch depended heavily on trade for a living, and one of their sources of income had been as the carrier of nearly all the salt used in Europe from the beds in the south of Portugal. When Spain disciplined the rebellious Netherlands by closing the salt pans to any but Portuguese shipping, the Dutch began to look for new sources.

These were found around 1600 on the coast of Venezuela, and the Dutch ships began calling regularly. To make the long voyage more profitable, they carried manufactured goods from Europe on the outward journey, trading them to the Spanish Caribbean islands. After twenty years of bickering, Spain recognized Dutch independence in 1621, and the Dutch immediately set up the Dutch West India Company.

At about the same time, the British and French turned from their preoccupation with European power struggles and began to think of colonization abroad, particularly in the Caribbean, where they could embarrass Spain. Thus the first settling of the Leeward Islands, so long ignored by Spain, had a distinctly anti-Spanish bias.

The Dutch settled St. Maarten, Saba, and St. Eustatius, or Statia, which for a hundred years was the busiest and richest free port in the Lesser Antilles. In 1624 the first English colony in the Caribbean was established on St. Kitts. A year later, the English began settling Barbados. The English and Dutch jointly occupied St. Croix in the Virgin Islands, Nevis was settled by English from St. Kitts, and other English soon moved into Montserrat. The French began settlements on Guadeloupe and Martinique.

The Dutch thought of colonies in terms of bases for raiding and smuggling among the Spanish islands. Their stepped-up naval campaign all but wiped Spanish ships from the Caribbean. Their attacks strained the over-taxed resources of Spain almost to the breaking point, making it easier for other nations to settle

unoccupied Caribbean islands without serious danger of Spanish interference. This danger was lessened even more when Piet Heyn, in command of 31 Dutch ships, surprised and captured the Spaniards' homebound flotilla off Mantanzas, seizing booty worth 15 million guilders and wrecking Spanish credit in Europe.

Colonies of other nations helped the Dutch in two ways. Every new colony meant more shipping for Dutch fleets, for the British and French had not yet built up their maritime power. And the Dutch had learned how to grow sugar.

In fact, the Dutch became the founders of the sugar industry in the British and French West Indies. They had acquired the know-how in Brazil. They were prepared to advance the necessary capital. They could supply the equipment needed from Europe. As the prime carriers in the West Indies, it was to their advantage to encourage the production of any big-money crop for which there was demand in Europe. And they even moved to provide the necessary cheap labor by seizing most of the Portuguese slave barracoons in West Africa. The Dutch now had an abundant supply of slaves and were anxious to sell them to the new sugar industry they were fostering.

Sugar and slavery changed the economy and the society of the West Indies. In the middle of the 1640s, white population in all the islands reached its peak and rapidly declined, never to recover. By the middle of the 1650s, fewer and fewer white men were controlling an increasingly large number of Africans, as sugar became the lifeblood, the very reason for existence, of the colonies in the Lesser Antilles.

Eventually the Dutch lost their control of the slave trade to the English. Both the English and the French governments passed laws restricting colonial trade to their own ships. By 1694 Dutch wars with England and France had damaged the Dutch West India Company's shipping, steadily diminishing trade had destroyed its income, and the once powerful company collapsed into bankruptcy.

As the 18th century opened, the English and French were mustering their forces for a struggle that was to bring fabulous wealth, and needless pillage and bloodshed, to the sun-blessed islands of the Lesser Antilles. And to leave a legacy of a hodge-podge of allegiances and societies that still intrigue and reward but also bedevil the traveler today.

ANTIGUA

With an international airport, a year-round warm, dry climate, and shores of bays with white sand beaches, Antigua is a resort area and the point of entry to the Lesser Antilles for many visitors. Antigua (pronounced Anteega with a hard 'g') is also part of the Caribbean defense network, a role it has played for two hundred years.

At their greatest dimensions, Antigua's 108 square miles are only 13 miles long by 9 miles wide, but Columbus managed to find the island on his second voyage in 1493. At various times during the following century, Spaniards and Frenchmen dropped by. They didn't stay, apparently considering the island too dry (it has an average rainfall of 45 inches). Possibly because their own weather has made them indifferent to the eccentricities of other climates, the Englishmen who came over from nearby St. Kitts in 1632 liked what they saw and settled on Antigua. The forests that had originally covered the island were cut back to the mountain tops and before very long sugar began raising its tasseled head. A rather mixed bag of Frenchmen, Irish malcontents, and Caribs seized the island in 1666. It was returned to the English in the following year and has been English ever since.

Although sugar has always been important, the island's strategic location and the bays around it have interested English naval officers. When England and France began their fight for control of the Lesser Antilles at the beginning of the 18th century, English Harbor, on southeastern Antigua, became the base for England's Caribbean squadrons. It was here that young Horatio Nelson came, near the end of the century, to command the dockyard that now bears his name.

More and more visitors find ideal loafing in Antigua. There is only one hotel on each bay and most of them are comparatively new. The rainfall is light and the humidity is low. As the island is fairly flat, trade winds air-condition nearly all of it every day.

The weather that makes Antigua ideal for visitors has raised hob with the lives of the residents, however. The rainfall is not only light, it's undependable; some years drought has all but ruined the sugar harvest. Antigua's dry climate, and the nature of its soil, account for the frequent appearances throughout the island of the *century plant and the cactus*, shown at the right.

Antigua played a role in Caribbean defense during the Second World War, too. When England needed ships in 1940, she received 50 over-age destroyers from America in return for 99-year leases for military bases on British possessions. One of these bases was on Antigua.

There's still a NASA tracking station on the island, but most of the American forces have long since gone. Before they left, they turned over their airfield to Antigua. This has now become a terminal for big jets from Europe and America, as well as for the two airlines that provide daily service throughout the Lesser Antilles. This easy communication has been a major factor in changing life for all the islands. Until the post-war air age, there was little direct travel between the islands, and travel to the outside world depended heavily on the unscheduled appearances of freighters.

Looking north from near the "center" of Antigua, (above) on the Sea View Farm Road, west of All Saints, showing two of the three distinct land formations of Antigua. The harbor and capital *city of St. John's* (top, right) looking north from Grey's Hill. The twin silver towers are part of the cathedral. To the left, a tall stack marks the 300-acre site of the oil refinery at Friar's Hill. Single-masted fishing sloops can get into *St. John's harbor* (lower left), although they often send their cargo ashore in lighters such as that shown *unloading bananas at the market sea wall* (lower right).

There have never been any difficulties in landing on Antigua, though, for the *birds on a salt pond* back of Galley Bay, shown overleaf.

In the late afternoon, a yacht meanders toward St. John's across *Hawksbill Bay* (top, left), as the lowering sun glints the surf whishing lazily along the quiet beach of *Galley Bay* (above).

Inland, north of Falmouth Harbor, two boys on donkeys are on *the road into Liberta* (far left), one of the villages settled by the slaves after their emancipation in 1834.

The best of both worlds—or bays—belongs to guests at a *south coast resort* (center, left) on a neck of land between Carlisle Bay in the foreground and Morris Bay beyond.

Silk Cotton Tree on Fig Tree Hill (left), in the heart of Antigua's rain forest, southeast of Boggy Peak. If the wind blows when the tree is in bloom, the valley below is littered with "cotton".

One of the many Caribbean beaches along Antigua's west coast.

Nelson's Dockyard in English Harbor as seen from Shirley Heights. Even today yachts sailing the Caribbean sometimes have difficulty finding the entrance, off to the left, so effectively is it screened by overlapping necks of land.

Captain Horatio Nelson was 25 when he arrived to assume command of English Harbor in 1784. His orders were to stop the illicit trading of American merchant ships in the Leeward Islands. He stopped the trade and incensed the residents. They neither called on him nor received him.

However, he found companionship on nearby Nevis, where in 1787 he married Frances Nisbet. The bride was given away by Nelson's friend and brother-officer, Prince William Henry, Duke of Clarence, later King William IV. That same year he completed his tour at English Harbor.

Nelson saw Antigua only once again, in early June of 1805, when he was searching for Napoleon's fleet. He found it at Trafalgar, and Nelson's victory there eliminated the main purpose of the naval base he had helped to strengthen at English Harbor.

It is hot up here on the Ridge, hot and bare and dry. The views are delightful, such as that *eastward toward Marmora Bay* (lower left). The Caribbean is beautiful. The trade winds blow, but the land is dusty and hard underfoot and the spare vegetation is fibrous and thorny.

The *military ruins* (above) are a utilitarian product of the age that produced one of Europe's most civilized styles of architecture, the Georgian. What remains suggests that like most Georgian architecture, they were solid, sensible, and pleasingly proportioned.

Their present state of ruin began with an earthquake in 1843. Waterloo had earlier destroyed their purpose. During 1854–55 the last of the troops were withdrawn.

Going down the *road to the Ridge* (right) you pass more of the empty military shells. Through the thorny lattices of one of their casements you can look eastwards to the *NASA tracking station* (above) at Dow Hill.

Where telescopes once searched the horizon for sails, a sensitive antenna now picks up sounds thousands of light years away. As long as they don't interfere with operations, animals graze among the equipment on the 600-acre base. This was a condition of the lease to the Americans by the Antiguans.

Antigua acquired the Dockyard in 1906, after it had ceased to be of use to the Royal Navy. The abandoned Dockyard decayed until the Society of the Friends of English Harbor, formed in 1951, undertook the restoration program that has made Nelson's Dockyard one of the most rewarding historical sites in the Antilles.

Clarence House (above) was built for the arrival of the Duke of Clarence in 1787, and is now the country residence of the governor.

The full sweep of the restored *Nelson's Dockyard from Clarence House* (right) is our final view of Antigua. Dockyard restoration has been accompanied by increasing use of the area as a base by international yachtsmen, so that English Harbor is enjoying a new — and much more peaceful — life.

(Below) A slip beside the *pillars of the old sail loft*.

GUADELOUPE

Even on a map, Guadeloupe (a department of France) conveys something of the irrational poetry of the tropics, being shaped like a giant green butterfly. It is really two islands; a low, big island and a high, "lower" island that are separated by a river that is not a river at all.

At the southern end of the outer islands of the Lesser Antilles, the eastern island of Guadeloupe is a comparatively flat limestone plateau whose highest hills rise no more than 300 feet above sea level. Its 250-square-mile area is about 100 square miles smaller than its sister island, yet it is called Grande Terre, or great land.

The western island is one of the chain of young volcanoes that comprise most of the Lesser Antilles. It is named Basse Terre (low land) apparently because it is below, or to the lee of . . . but let's not go into *that* again.

Separating these two islands is Rivière Salée, which is not really a river at all. It is a canal or tidal channel, 4 miles long and from 50 to 70 yards wide, between the Atlantic and the Caribbean.

The low hills of Grande Terre are covered with sugar cane. It is still carried to mills as shown by the *bullock cart on a bridge near Morne-à-l'Eau* (above).

Trucks, such as the one nuzzling the bullock cart, carry the processed sugar to Pointe-à-Pitre.

This is the *waterfront of Pointe-à-Pitre*, Guadeloupe's main port. The inter-island schooners are unloading along the sea wall across from the Place de la Victoire. Beyond them is the open air market, a fragrant, noisy place such as is found in every Lesser Antilles port.

Off the picture to the left is a large U-shaped area fringed by wharves for bigger freighters and ocean liners.

Guadeloupe's largest city, Pointe-à-Pitre, is on Grande Terre, just east of the Rivière Salée. About one-third the size of Pointe-à-Pitre, Guadeloupe's capital is the city of Basse Terre, on the opposite side of the island of the same name.

In 1654 a sailor named Pieters landed with Dutch families who had been driven out of Brazil. Apparently he settled on the point of land now surrounded by wharves. In time this became known as Pointe-à-Pieters. The settlement at the inlet was the village of Morne Renferme.

English forces invaded Guadeloupe in 1691 and 1703, but it was their occupancy from 1759 to 1763, during the Seven Years War, that changed the fortunes of Guadeloupe and put it on the road to prosperity. Quick to see the advantages of this natural harbor, the English did much to develop it. This development was continued after the war by the French, who in 1769 officially named it Pointe-à-Pitre.

The 18th century wars in the Caribbean between the English and French have already been mentioned. They will be mentioned again, for they played a decisive role in making the Lesser Antilles what they are today. It seems only fair, then, to warn you that in the 113 years between 1702 and 1815, England and France fought five major wars covering a total of 56 years in which the Lesser Antilles were closely involved.

At the end of the Seven Years War, for example, Britain had occupied Guadeloupe, Martinique, Dominica, St. Lucia, St. Vincent, Grenada, and Tobago, as well as her own Leeward Islands, Barbados and Trinidad. Had she kept them all, they might today be united culturally and economically as well as politically. As it was, larger pawns were at stake; many of the islands were returned to France, and the Lesser Antilles continued to be controlled and divided by rival metropolitan governments.

Their peoples today are struggling to make a coherent life out of this fragmented legacy.

Easternmost point of Guadeloupe, *la Pointe des Châteaux* (above) is the ragged remnant of volcanic spikes. Guadeloupe has five dependencies: Désirade, St. Barthélemy, St. Martin, Marie Galante, and Les Saintes.

Viewed from a sort of moat around its landward side is the entrance to Fort Fleur d'Epée.

Fishermen returning to Désirade, half a dozen miles from Guadeloupe.

The Gates of Hell on the eastern side of the northern apex of Grande Terre. Outside, the Atlantic snarls and roars, sending waves crashing through the entrance, where they break their backs and slide submissively to a small beach at the head of the sheltered inlet.

Empty conch shells piled along the marketplace quai
in Pointe-à-Pitre.

Fishermen cracking conch shells on Petit Canal.

Four charming examples of the traditional Creole costumes known as the "madras" and "foulard". It is a style blended of elements from 18th century France, Spain, Africa, and India.

Church in Pointe-à-Pitre, nicknamed "The Iron Cathedral" because it contains iron girders criss-crossed and bolted firmly against earthquakes.

Balconies showing some of the iron grill work once characteristic of French colonial architecture.

Lighthouse Island with its two public beaches, as seen from
Guadeloupe's Gosier Beach. Dominica lies under the clouds in the
distance. Between the two islands was fought in 1782 the battle
that destroyed French naval power in the Caribbean and left
Britain's Royal Navy supreme.

Seafood displayed on beach-chair (left) was caught by a skin-diving visitor to the beach near Gosier (above).

(Overleaf) School is out at the beach of Anse Laborde, Grande Terre.

La Capricieuse (the capricious one) the islanders call *Soufrière Volcano* (right), because of the seemingly willful way it hides behind the clouds and then unexpectedly reveals its coronetted crater, like a flirt manipulating a fan. Early morning is the best time to catch it off guard before it has enveloped its top in clouds.

The top of Soufrière is 4,813 feet above sea level, the highest point in Guadeloupe and one of the higher points in the Lesser Antilles. Its last major eruption was in 1797, although it has spouted off now and then through the years until as recently as 1956. Soufrière's main activity is confined to the sulphur vents from which it gets its name.

Soufrière does pour torrents down its side, not of lava, but of life-giving water from its cloud-sponged heights. One of the most breath-taking of these is *Les Chutes du Carbet* (Carbet Falls) (left) on the eastern side of Soufrière.

Near the falls, a little south of it, is the *Grand Etang* (below), a freshwater wildlife refuge where ducks can add mullet to their menu.

Set serenely in the midst of the old family crypts in its graveyard
is *St. Joseph's Church* (above) in the town of Vieux-Habitants, on the
west coast of Basse Terre. This parish was founded in 1639, four years
after the French began colonizing Guadeloupe. The first church
building on this site was built as early as 1666.

The Arawak Indians were entirely wiped out about twenty years after Columbus first met them on the island of Hispaniola. But it was not the first time this people had suffered at the hands of others. Archaeological excavations suggest, for instance, that they lived on Guadeloupe as early as 200 A.D., and that somewhere around the year 1000, Caribs from the South American mainland arrived and either killed them or drove them north. One group of Indians or the other, and opinion seems to favor the Arawaks, carved the *Indian petroglyphs* (top, left) near the village of Trois Rivières, on the southern tip of Basse Terre.

Basse Terre is an island. It is also a city. The city is Guadeloupe's capital and second port. From the waterfront market you can look across the downtown area, to the hills above the city where the government officials and businessmen have their homes, then beyond to the distant view of *Soufrière from Basse Terre* (lower left).

Although it is more of a roadstead than a sheltered harbor, Basse Terre has been growing in importance as a port. Construction of port facilities that can handle ocean liners was begun in 1962. Priority was given to the pier designed for the speedy, *safe loading of banana boats* (below). For while the sugar of Grande Terre remains Guadeloupe's most important agricultural export, Basse Terre, like so many of the other fertile, high islands, is plumping its economy by growing acres of bananas.

And, too, a port that can berth ocean liners is always helpful to an island that is discovering tourism as more visitors each year discover Guadeloupe. With the scenery and climate of the Lesser Antilles, Guadeloupe is an attractive place to visit, and most of its resorts are comparatively new and quite comfortable. But it is *les bons gens de la Guadeloupe* who make the real difference, their verve and hospitality warming a visit into a delightful memory.

DOMINICA

"Typical Dominica" they say. They mean that Dominica is the largest of the British Windward Islands but it has the smallest population, and many of its people emigrate to make a living. Until 1940 it was classed as a Leeward Island. A British island, it is sandwiched between two French islands. Its people speak a patois that boasts a vocabulary of obsolete French with an African grammar. Dominica is an ideal place for growing citrus fruits, but disease swept its lime plantations and then synthetic citrus acid was developed. The natural location for a coaling station when the Panama Canal was built, Dominica lost out to St. Lucia because its harbor was not developed. When the United States and Britain blockaded nearby Guadeloupe and Martinique because they opted for the Vichy government after the fall of France during the Second World War, thousands of the French islanders fled to Dominica, with the result that the island's food resources were drained so badly it took several years to recover after the war.

"Typical Dominica". Even when things seem to be going its way, almost inevitably something happens to mess them up. That is what its residents, with wry humor, refer to as "typical Dominica".

It is hoped that the days of "typical Dominica" are drawing to a close. Its beauty is stunning and it boasts a remarkably healthy climate. These facts, combined with daily air service, are bringing visitors to Dominica's shores in increasing numbers. And once visitors have seen Dominica it tends to stick strongly in their memory.

Dominica is the most mountainous island in the Lesser Antilles, boasting the highest mountains in the chain. Morne Diablotin rises to 4,500 feet above the sea, and there is always a bundle of clouds perched atop it. This situation creates a landmark visible for a great many miles out to sea, which in the days of sail made Dominica a favored landfall.

Clouds mean rain, even in the Lesser Antilles. On the sheltered, lee side of the island, rainfall averages 80 inches a year, while in the mountainous interior it rises to 250 inches a year. There are few wide valleys to absorb this moisture, so the rain tears down to the sea in a host of rivers—they say there is one for every day in the year, 365 in all.

The rain and fertile soil give Dominica an authentic rain forest, tall and cool and lush, covering three-quarters of its 305 square miles; only about 15 per cent of the island is cultivated.

The mountainous terrain makes road-building difficult and expensive; some roads are simply not attempted. For instance, there is no road over the 20 miles between the island's natural harbor, Portsmouth, and its capital, Roseau. A round-about route covering 50 miles connects them; on the way, this road passes through the airport which is on the east coast, about a forty-five minute drive from Roseau even though the island is only 16 miles wide (it is 29 miles long). Portsmouth likely was considered too malarial an area. Malaria has long since been controlled, but Roseau remains the capital.

Dominica's mountains have played another important role in the island's development. Because they left little flat land, the sugar cane industry could not be developed on the island, sparing Dominica the heritage of slavery that is so marked on many of the other West Indian islands. Today, many of Dominica's inhabitants are independent landowners, farming small plots for a modest income. (Their patois, which they share with St. Lucia, developed as a result of frequent French occupation of the islands in the 18th century. It has so changed over the years that today's French people cannot understand it.) There is yet another strain in Dominica's population: it has provided a refuge for the increasingly harassed Caribs. There is, however, dispute as to how many are left, figures ranging from two thousand to none of pure Carib blood.

The need to recover from an irrational succession of frustrations throughout their history seems to have developed in the people of Dominica an out-going friendliness and cheerfulness that contributes greatly to the pleasure of a visit. There is an increasing number of people who feel that "typical Dominica" may soon cease to mean just perverse luck and come instead to mean a special blend of happy friendship, beauty, and pleasure.

In the heart of Dominica's rain forest, trees soar up to 120 feet. Giant ferns shimmer up the mountainside along the road like festival banners along a parade route. Sun and shadow shatter the single color green into thousands of variations, relieved by occasional spots of color such as the *hibiscus* (right).

Here you find the *stands of gommier trees* (above) whose hard, handsome wood is now being felled by a Canadian firm for use as a veneer in furniture making. Measuring up to 7 feet in diameter, the gommiers (French for "gum trees") yield a sap that, when dry, blazes up like tinder and is used by the natives to light fires.

The *carrapid trees* (opposite) are even harder than gommiers; they will break the axe used in trying to chop them.

Rarely can any member of a vanishing race have looked as healthy and handsome as the *Carib mother and child* (above). There are few, if any, pure Caribs left. The survivors are of mixed Carib and Negro blood, but their features are still predominantly those of ancestors who came from Venezuela and, at a far more distant time, from ancient Asia.

Caribs held Dominica against white invaders for two and a half centuries after its discovery. As warriors they were fierce, brave, and hungry. From them we get not only *Caribbees* and *Caribbean*, but by way of *caribal* and *canibal*, the word *cannibal*. In the middle of the 16th century they listed their preferences among Europeans as French (delicious), English, Dutch, and Spanish. This may well be the ultimate tribute to French cuisine.

The Carib language also gave us *hurricane* and *savannah*; its *kanaua* went through the Spanish *canoa* to become our *canoe*. But the *Carib canoe* (opposite, top left) remained their own, which they still make and sell to island fishermen.

The Carib canoe is made from a single gommier log, felled during a new moon to prevent rot. It is hollowed out with an adz. Then the ends are trussed and the canoe is filled with stones and water to widen the center. Low fires burn under it and the sides are kept wide with sticks. When this is finished the inside of the hull is ribbed and cross-braced, and the sides are heightened with planks that converge into a cutting edge along the bow.

In 1903 the Caribs were granted about 3,000 acres

along 8 miles of the Atlantic coast as a reservation. About a thousand Caribs live there now. The road in climbs the hills above *Hattan Garden Bay* (right, bottom) to Salybia, their main settlement: a police station, a school, and the church of St. Marie des Caribes. The church has an overturned *Carib canoe as the altar* (top, far right). From Salybia, it's a hot hike, uphill all the way, to the village of the present Carib chief, who is an elected official.

They used to live in high, roomy *carbets*, with an upper floor for sleeping. Today Caribs live in two-room houses. The present chief, Jermandois Francis, is in the light hat and sports shirt, supervising the villagers *repairing a Carib house* (center).

Trafalgar Falls (above), at the head of Roseau Valley.
From here the river flows down to the sea through a
valley where massive, succulent oranges and grapefruit
dangle temptingly on trees along the roadside.

   In warm, wet areas of this leeward coast lives the
crapaud (bottom, far left), a frog that weighs about two
pounds and is served by the islanders as a delicacy they
call "mountain chicken".

   High in the inaccessible areas of the mountain
there are still examples of the *Sisserou* (bottom, near
left) or Imperial Parrot. Found only on Dominica, it is
the largest parrot on the island. Two of them support
the crest on Dominica's coat of arms.

From the ruins of a fort on the heights of Morne
Bruce, we look across the capital city and port of
Roseau (top, left). The white ship stands off the
main port facilities. In the foreground are the 44
acres of the Botanical Garden. Established in 1891,
its spacious grounds are considered by many to
be the most beautiful botanical garden in the
West Indies. The building with the silver roof is
a shopping center.

Down in the heart of town, where Turkey
Lane runs into Queen Mary Street, is the *Convent
Local Handicrafts* (right, center) operated by Sister
Mary Bertine and Sister Mary Camille of the
Missionary Sisters of the Immaculate Heart of Mary.
It was established in 1950 by Sister Mary Bertine
to provide a source of income for island girls who do
not want to go into domestic service.

The mats are woven of "khus-khus" grass.
(In Jamaica the roots of this grass are used to make
perfume.) The small individual sections are made
by younger girls at home, or by these girls
during slack periods.

Leaving town and heading inland we have
this view of *Roseau Valley* (bottom, left) with
Morne Trois Pitons in the background. In the
foreground are neat rows of trees in a lime grove,
sheltered by eucalyptus trees.

Far up the valley, south of Trafalgar Falls,
are the *sulphur springs* (bottom, right) that give
pungent evidence of volcanic activity still
muttering below Dominca's green and wet surface.

Back down to Roseau and going north
along the leeward coast, we cross the bridge that
provides this view of the mouth of the *Layou River*
(top, right) with the Caribbean beyond.

(Above) *From the road leading over the hump to the airport on the Atlantic coast, we pause to look back for one last glimpse at the high mountains of Dominica.*

(Top, left) *The village of Soufrière with the silver-roofed buildings of a lime juice factory.*

(Bottom, left) *A girl relaxes on Mero Beach while a man cuts up whitefish for chub.*

MARTINIQUE

Madinina. Madinina. Madinina—"island of flowers", the Caribs called it. Martinique is still an island of flowers with many cartons of them going to the florists of Paris. It's an island of coffee and *cafe au lait* beauty. It's an island where carnival lasts six weeks and Cole Porter found the beguine he began. Yet, for all its quick, bright glamor as the place where the gaiety of Paris and the gusto of Africa have melded, Martinique is a reserved island, quietly conscious of its past.

It was a comparatively late starter, not being discovered by Columbus until 1502. The French arrived in 1625 and were met by the Caribs. Their resistance to the French was aided by the rain-forest wilderness and mountainous terrain that even today comprises much of Martinique's 425 square miles.

The forces of sugar and slavery were the same as they were in the other islands until Martinique was captured by the English in 1794. They occupied the island until 1800; Martinique was not officially returned to France until 1815.

During this time Martinique was sheltered from the upheaval and bloodshed of the revolution that swept France and changed Guadeloupe. The colony survived intact, but many of the leaders lost their families and all of them lost the society that had nurtured them. From then on Martinique was their home; there was no other.

They evolved a cultured society centered around St. Pierre. The eruption that buried St. Pierre in 1903 wiped out a glittering society and slowed the heart of Martinique to a somber beat.

Island plantations and businesses remain in the hands of descendants of the old families. Negroes still find most of their employment on plantations, although bananas are vying with sugar as the main export crop. Several thousand islanders fish the sea for a living, often selling their catch right at the shore, as these *fishermen at St. Anne* (left) are doing.

Whatever their occupation, social status, or skin color, the people of Martinique do have an air of reserve, noticeable even to a casual visitor. With patience and courtesy, this same visitor can discover, to his great pleasure, that the French tradition of good living still reaches full flower in the tropical beauty of Martinique.

Through the centuries the French have developed a connoisseur's appreciation of the pleasure of irony. Doubtless it was a source of refined amusement to them that their two islands in the Lesser Antilles profited immensely from being captured by the British.

The capture, prosperity, and return of Guadeloupe have already been mentioned. That was in 1763. From then until the Revolution, France's sugar islands in the Antilles enjoyed their golden age.

Although the French were later in getting started than the English, French sugar production was ahead of that of the English islands. It stayed ahead during the golden decades. The French, moreover, concentrated on the production of white, semi-refined sugar, rather than the wet, brown muscavado of the British islands.

The planters prospered, but the other settlers found themselves more and more on the sidelines. Sugar was a rich man's crop. It required money to finance the building of a sugar factory and required money to buy and work the large amount of land needed to justify a factory. By the second half of the 18th century many of the *petits blancs* on Martinique, descendants of the poor Normans and Bretons who had settled the island, were off the land and formed a middle class in the island's main settlements.

More and more of the land was in the hands of fewer and fewer families. Their life was in the cities, particularly St. Pierre. Whether chatting in the fountain-cooled gardens of St. Pierre or sweating on the plains of Lamentin, the planters dreamed of the day they could return to France, if only for a holiday. When they did, their visits made "rich as a Creole"

synonymous with wealth.

Few of them returned to France in 1793. The Revolution toppled the throne. France and Britain began a state of war that continued until 1815, with the exception of a brief interlude from 1801 to 1803.

Both countries sent fleets to the Caribbean. The British forces were welcomed by the French royalists on Martinique.

As they had done earlier on Guadeloupe, the British remained aloof from the internal affairs of Martinique. French laws continued as they were. Businesses and plantations were not touched. Proclamations from Paris had no effect; slaves remained slaves. And, with access to the British sugar market, it was the turn of the Martinique planters to prosper.

During the 1801-1803 intermission, Martinique was returned to the control of the metropolitan government of France, then under Napoleon. Among more pressing reasons, the event was of interest to Martinique because Napoleon's wife was a local girl. She was Marie Joseph Rose Tascher de la Pagerie,

sometimes known as Yeyette, best known as Josephine.

The *statue of the Empress Josephine* (top left) stands in the center of the Savane, a tree-fringed park area in the heart of Fort-de-France. From her pedestal she gazes across the water to the village of Trois Ilets, where she was baptized in 1763. There are the ruins of La Pagerie, her family home. Diagonally downhill, on the other side of the road, are the *ruins of the sugar factory at La Pagerie* (above), its chimney poking unsteadily into the sky, the rusted remains of a boiling-kettle against the wall, and an old-fashioned bullock cart resting in its yard.

After 1803 the British returned and stayed, off and on, until 1815. The Treaty of Vienna wrote an end to the 18th century squabbles and assigned the Lesser Antilles to allegiances that have lasted pretty well to this day.

Martinique went back to France, secure in the government, laws, and social structure of 1763. It was the old Martinique, the same Martinique; but it was a different France and a different world.

Martinique had been sheltered by the British occupation for almost a quarter of a century. Its laws and life had gone on unchanged. There had been no revolutionary cries in the streets and no killing. The slaves had not been freed. Business had prospered. The island was still in the hands of a few established families.

When they returned to France it was a strange land. Their old friends were either dead or poverty-stricken. The court was an assembly of bourgeois tradesmen. The political revolution had been established and the industrial revolution was under way. The streets were crowded, the crowds were rude, and the climate was bleak.

It was better among the green hills of home. Martinique was home. Here they stayed. Planters invested their profits in the island home, and the old, established families intermarried. They kept alive a society that was, for them, gracious and cultured.

They could turn their backs on Europe, but they could not stop the growing threat of two European developments of their sheltered years: the rights of man and the sugar beet. Both hit Martinique with full force in the 1840's.

To deal with the lesser one first, it was in the middle of the 18th century that a German scientist discovered the high sugar content of a beet that could be grown in temperate climates. Nothing much was done about this until the British blockage of his ports forced Napoleon to develop substitute foods. After the emergency and Napoleon had passed, the French continued to work on the development of the sugar beet industry. By 1830 it was established; by 1840 it was ready to sweep the market. A mixture of government price support, overproduction, rising prices, and consumer resistance soon produced a glut of sugar on the world market. This came at the time when Martinique was faced with the greatest crisis in its history: the emancipation of the slaves.

Other nations had banned the slave trade during the first few years of the century; France did so in 1818. In 1822, 1824, and 1833 slave revolts in Martinique forced the government to improve the slaves' conditions. It was already late and time was running out. In 1834 the British government abolished slavery in all its colonies. In that same year a French abolition society was formed that succeeded in getting an emancipation act proposed to the national assembly in 1838. The bill was not passed, and for ten years the debate continued. It ended in 1848 with the freeing of the slaves in the French colonies, largely through the courageous persistence of one man.

Victor Schoelcher was a French deputy from Alsatia. For much of his political career and most of his adult life he was a dedicated abolitionist. Today his name is revered in the French islands. The statue of *Victor Schoelcher* (below) stands in front of the Palais de Justice.

(Overleaf) *The Pitons du Carbet loom over deBriant Church, which is patterned after Sacre Coeur in Montmartre. It is near Balata, a town in the hills north of Fort-de-France on the road to Morne Rouge.*

From Fort-de-France the road north to Morne Rouge slashes and weaves through Martinique's rain forest area. On one side of the road, you can look down on giant bamboos growing up to you from the valley below; on the other side red-clawed heliconias scamper uphill between the legs of more stately and mature forest veterans.

In these luxuriant surroundings, *anthuriums* (left) cover acres on the Bonne plantation. Their colors range from white through subtle pinks deep into the most intense reds. Their growth is sheltered in the shade of gliricidia trees until they are ready to be picked for shipment to florists in Europe.

Northern Martinique is lush and green and, for the most part, steep. It is made up of the two mountain masses of the *Pitons du Carbet* (top, right) and *Mont Pelée*, the narrow strip of coastal plain around each, and the fertile highland between them.

On this rolling land that cuts across the island south of Morne Rouge, grow the small delicately sweet pineapples of Martinique. Grapefruit trees climb the hillsides, and banana plants crowd the cool, moist valleys.

On Martinique's Caribbean shore is the town of *St. Pierre*, with *Mont Pelée* (bottom, right) brooding in the background.

On the road just north of St. Pierre is the *Blue Madonna* (center, right), a shrine for fishermen who set out daily from these shores.

Somewhere on the hills around St. Pierre there was once a hut that housed Paul Gauguin for several months during the summer and fall of 1887. Here he found the subtleties of Impressionism inadequate. The intense colors and strong contrasts of light and shade, the luxuriant variety of the land, and the somber beauty of the people opened his eyes to a new path that was to lead to Tahiti, the Marquesas, and immortality.

All this is long past. It is difficult, now, to realize that this quiet little fishing village was once the prettiest and the gayest city in the Antilles, or that the slumbering green mountain in the background once burst open with a fiery fury that destroyed St. Pierre.

Within two or three minutes, sometime between 7:50 and 8:00 a.m. on Thursday, May 8, 1902, the city of St. Pierre and its 30,000 residents ceased to exist.

The most numbing volcanic tragedy of modern times destroyed a civilization that was distinctive, and. a city that was unique. Neither can be duplicated. St. Pierre was justly called the "little Paris of the Antilles".

Here French culture and Creole hospitality ripened to maturity under tropic skies. Wars and trade went through the fortified harbor of the island's capital, Fort Royal (renamed Fort-de-France after the Revolution). In St. Pierre things were easier and gayer; there was time for laughter and leisurely conversation and the whispers of dalliance.

In their homes, families and their guests would linger all afternoon over the four-hour Sunday dinner, a form of hospitality still shared in Martinique. In the morning they might have attended the services at the *church overlooking the Caribbean* (whose broken remnants are shown above), lingering to chat with friends on the wide steps leading to the street below where their carriages waited.

During the season there were performances at the theater. Audiences lingered to gossip in the *theater foyer* (opposite, top left).

For months there had been warnings from Mont Pelée. A carpet of fine gray ash had been laid over the land to the north of St. Pierre. Later a river of molten mud had buried a plantation and 150 of its workers in the same area. Pelée continued to emit steam and

smoke. There had been a shower of ashes over St. Pierre on May 7th, when the city received news of the eruption of Soufrière to the south on St. Vincent Island.

The governor sought to assure them that nothing was wrong by bringing his family to St. Pierre for the festival day.

The morning was cool under clear skies of blue. As the morning of May 8th ticked on, St. Pierre was quiet. Shops and businesses were closed for its *jour de fête*. In their homes, excited children rushed through breakfast, eager to begin the day's fun. Their amused parents lingered over coffee.

The entire side of Mont Pelée suddenly gaped. From it a massive torrent of fire roared down across the city and over the harbor. There was no lava. The eruption was gas, fire, and ash. The gas killed, the fire destroyed, the ash buried. Within three minutes it was all over. Trade winds began to clear away the sulphurous fumes. Below them was what had been a city.

From all of St. Pierre there was not a sound.

Years later this *statue in the theater ruins* (opposite) was commissioned to represent St. Pierre being reborn. Although she faces distant Mont Pelée, visible between the trees, her eyes are closed and her head is turned slightly in the direction of the sea, as though averted from looking directly at her destroyer. The spirit of the statue is gallant, but the face tells more of the truth. Another city may rise on this site, but what died at St. Pierre will never return. It is lost to us, forever.

West Indian Market in Fort-de-France is shown in three of the pictures above. This is on the west side of the city, along the Rivière Levassor. It is held every Saturday morning, when small farmers bring produce in from the surrounding countryside.

As much as anything else, the Saturday market is a chance for farmers from the country area to get together and exchange news or just plain gossip, and to see a bit of the city later in the day. Saturday afternoon and Sunday also mean *coq* fights in Martinique. You can usually spot a *coq* pit, even in the country, by the number of cars parked in the vicinity.

This one is on the eastern outskirts of Fort-de-France. The picture above shows the *coqs being weighed in* before the fights.

(Top, left) *Diamond Rock, a 600-foot high, mile-round boulder that for 17 months was fortified and commissioned as a sloop in the British Navy to harass the French during 1804 and 1805.*

(Top, right) *Village and beach of Diamant, a popular fishing and swimming area.*

(Bottom, right) *Rivière Pilote Valley in the southern part of Martinique.*

(Bottom, left) *Bay north of Ste. Marie in northern Martinique.*

Fort-de-France, looking southward over the harbor from Calvary Hill.

Looking north along the Rivière Levassor from a bridge along the waterfront.

(Left) *Fishermen at Bellefontaine haul in a net bursting with coulicou, a small fish like a sprat. Further north towards St. Pierre is the village of Carbet. It was here that Columbus came ashore on Martinique.*

(Below) *Fishing village of Grand Rivière.*

ST. LUCIA

Residents of St. Lucia pronounce it 'San LOOsha''.
It probably doesn't matter much since the original form
was probably St. Alouise or St. Aluoziel, the name
given to the island by the Spaniards who discovered it
somewhere between 1502 and 1509.

There's no disputing the rightness of the Tourist
Board sobriquet for St. Lucia: "the Helen of the
Antilles". To begin with, St. Lucia produces what are
probably the prettiest girls in the Lesser Antilles.
There's much of the saucy minx about the island itself;
temperamental, full of variety, vacillating in her
affections, smouldering, and, of course, beautiful. (As
part of her woman's prerogative, St. Lucia has adopted
the Italian song *Santa Lucia* as her own.)

St. Lucia was hard to capture and expensive to
keep. The English and French tried for a hundred
years, but were beaten off by the Caribs. When one of
them did get possession, the other took it away. St.
Lucia changed hands fourteen times, which is something of a record even for the Lesser Antilles.

The British wanted it for its strategic location,
near the French islands, and for its harbor, Castries.
Since 1815 it has remained Britain's island.

One of the finest natural harbors in the Antilles,
Castries is sheltered and deep. Its ability to handle large
ships has helped St. Lucia's economy during periods
when other islands were depressed. Castries has also
become a haven for yachts sailing Caribbean waters.

Yachtsmen approaching St. Lucia from the south
make their landfall at one of the best-known landmarks
of the Lesser Antilles, the *Two Pitons* (left), south of
Soufrière. These cones rise sheerly from the sea to
heights of 2,619 feet for *Gros Piton* (left and 2,461 feet
for *Petit Piton* (right).

A lush and undulating land, St. Lucia has ripe hills
and fertile valleys that produce a varied agriculture.
Sugar has never dominated its economy, owing in part
to its vivacious history. Its French and English parent-
age has given St. Lucia a somewhat knowing air,
unexpected in an island so rich in unspoiled beauty.

Celebrated for its "frenetic dance steps", St. Lucia has some scenery that is pretty wild too, within the beguiling variety of its 233 square miles. Lying in a north-south direction for 27 miles, with a maximum width of 14 miles, St. Lucia is an island of volcanoes, both old and new.

From a comparative plain around Gros Islet, the northern half of the island rolls south over old, eroded volcanoes. This area contains wide, flat-bottomed valleys; the flattest are Roseau and Cul de Sac Valleys.

The southern half of the island consists of younger, steeper volcanoes with some life in them yet. After the island was formed, later volcanic eruptions filled in the valleys along their southern flanks, smoothing them out a bit to the broad plain that slopes down to the Vieux Fort area at the southern tip of St. Lucia.

In the southern mountains Soufrière still bubbles away. The *sulphur cauldrons of Soufrière* (below) are a tourist attraction and, it is hoped, a safety valve. Described as " a particularly well-behaved volcano" Soufrière has had one wedge of its crater so eroded that you can drive into it along a road above these pools. For a closer look at the pools, it is wise to secure the services of a guide.) Here you can see in action one phase of the volcanic activity that made these islands.

Soufrière volcano has a wide opening in its side above Soufrière Valley. At the other end, where the valley opens to the sea is the town of Soufrière, the

second largest on St. Lucia. Along its shore is the wide *beach at Soufrière* (above, right) with fishing nets drying in the foreground and the Pitons beyond.

St. Lucia is fortunate in having a terrain and a history that prevented sugar from ever dominating the island's economy. Sugar was, and is, grown here, but it is only one of several crops. Since 1954 bananas have

become the big crop in the British Windward Islands. Many of the planters on the islands are descendants of old families, and, having good memories, they know that any island that depends heavily on one crop is at the mercy of weather, demand, and price.

Fortunately, St. Lucia has always had a diversified agriculture. Much of it, though, has been for export. Small islands often do not have enough land to feed growing populations, so they concentrate on export crops to get the money needed for the food they import to feed their people. In the best of times it can be a narrow squeak to balance the income from exports with the expenses for imports. If times get bad, the islands suffer a trade deficit and even hunger.

Tourism has added another element. More and more visitors are "discovering" the restful beauty of these once almost forgotten islands. Growing tourism can provide an increasingly large income for an island, but visitors have to be fed. If the food is imported, the island loses a large piece of the money from tourism. If islanders can grow much of the needed food themselves, visitors dine well—very well, indeed—on fresh food and the money stays on the island, circulated among island residents to their benefit. Antigua is beginning to move in this direction. With its beautiful beaches and rich soil, St. Lucia can make especially good use of this economic possibility.

This digression was prompted by Soufrière Valley. The Valley is lovely in itself, and a restful, fascinating place to wander in. Much of its color comes from the variety of its growth. Much of this comes from efforts by Andre du Boulay to extend the island's income.

Mr. du Boulay is a planter and a businessman. He is descended from a family that has lived in this area for over three hundred years. He loves the land, the island, and its people. Much of our social thinking during the past thirty years or so has tended to overlook the fact that authority, first of all, means responsibility. Mr. du Boulay invests a large portion of his capital in extensive agricultural experiments. Some of them are short-range ones to increase the quality and productivity per acre of crops now raised in St. Lucia; others seek to discover if the island can successfully grow new crops, some of them high-income exports. If an experiment doesn't work out, he pays for it. If an experiment succeeds, he profits, there are more jobs and income for more island residents, and more taxes for the government.

On a hillside above Soufrière Valley, *the du Boulay home* (top, right) gives an appearance of belonging to the site, almost as though rising from it naturally. This effect is added to by the landscaping of the surrounding grounds with tropical plantings of the island. Strolling through these grounds, Mr. du Boulay discussed a problem that bedevils businessmen in all the islands — or anywhere else, for that matter. To market island products successfully, one must price them competitively. Competitive prices usually necessitate more efficient production. Efficiency often means more machines, but fewer jobs. And the crying need of these overpopulated islands is for enough jobs to go around. Mr. du Boulay raised his hands in the traditional French gesture of inquiry.

Although it may become a business, purely as a hobby Mr. du Boulay has been restoring the *Royal Mineral Baths in Soufrière Valley* (center, right, with Mr. du Boulay in the white shirt). These baths are not to be confused with the sulphur baths inside Soufrière crater. Samples of the water from the streams in this section of the valley were sent to France for analysis two centuries ago, and the water was found to be the equal of that in the restorative mineral baths in France. Louis XV ordered baths built for the refreshment of his troops stationed on St. Lucia. They were carved out of solid rock and were originally fed from an underground pipeline from a spring high in the hills.

One of the original baths is in the foreground, still overgrown as it has been for years. Behind it is the shelter built over two of the restored original baths and several new ones. The overflow tank is used as an outdoor pool. For now, they are used only by personal guests but they may be opened to the public in the future. As well as being very relaxing, the baths are rumored to be able to ease away the years and restore youthful vitality. The results should be interesting.

Back of the baths is a small valley that Mr. du Boulay deliberately left in its natural state, as a sort of domesticated jungle. At its head is a *fall of mineral water* (bottom, right) that has left a multi-hued stain on the rocks behind it.

A dessert of sliced bananas covered with coconut cream is delicious—and fattening. Bananas and coconuts go well together while they're growing, too. After the banana bunches are harvested, the decaying plants help create a richer soil for better, more productive coconut trees. In turn the coconut palms provide shelter that protects the growing banana plants from high winds and too much sun. As a result, the mixed *plantation of coconut palms and banana plants* (above) is appearing in greater numbers.

Where the palm fronds fan out directly from the trunk, nestle the *clusters of coconuts* (top, left). Ripe nuts are usually cut off before they fall. It's still quite a job to get at the white meat inside, whether you want to use it to eat or to make copra. In these pictures we're showing coconuts being processed for copra.

Coconut husking (top, right) is done by bringing the tree nut swiftly down onto a sharp point or edge, a spike or a cutlass or even a pointed stick of hard wood. From that gash, the husker tears off the outer shell, a coating of tightly packed fiber about two inches thick. He is after an object about the size of a hairy softball, as shown in this *pile of husked coconuts* (bottom, left). Most of the steps in *turning coconuts into copra* are shown in the photo (bottom, right).

The woman at the left is opening the nuts with a cutlass. The coconut water falls into the tub and the split nuts are tossed into a pile. The split nuts are then put into a kiln for roasting. There are two sides to the kiln; each side holds about 1000 nuts. Roasting takes about two days. Nuts are put in one side for a day. The next day the nuts on the other side are removed, and a fresh batch put in. And so on, month after month.

The roasting removes much of the water from the meat, causing it to shrink away from the shell. After the roasted meat has cooled sufficiently, the woman on the right uses a curved knife to scoop out the meat. The empty shells are used as fuel for the kiln.

The dried coconut meat is copra. It is bagged and shipped to the copra factory at Soufrière where the remaining water is removed and the copra is processed to extract a refined oil used for cooking and in the manufacture of soaps. The fiber residue is used as a component in animal feeds. Nothing is wasted.

Bananas on a tree (top, left) grow in what we would consider to be an upside-down position. The supporting plant is called a "trunk". The big bunch of bananas is called a "stem". On each stem the clusters are called "hands" and the individual bananas are called "fingers".

Banana plants grow from cuttings or shoots of earlier plants. From the planting to the harvesting of a stem ready for shipping takes from 8 to 10 months. After the stem has been harvested, the trunk that bore it is cut down to leave room for another trunk to grow from the same planting. Planters usually grow only two or three trunks from each planting; then they dig up their fields and replant.

Bananas are sold by the pound, with mature stems averaging between 40 to 60 pounds each. After cutting, bananas are carried by head, as shown in this picture of *boys heading bananas* (bottom, left) to a banana-buying point along the roadside. To these small, banana-leaf shelters come the trucks of the Banana Growers Association. They weigh and buy the bananas and carry them to either of the ports of Castries or Vieux Fort, where the bananas are purchased by Geest Industries and shipped in their refrigerated freighters to Britain.

Bananas need water and shelter from the wind. The water can come from rainfall or irrigation, the shelter can be provided by coconut trees or valley walls. The plants usually have to be sprayed to prevent leaf spot disease. The ripening stems are protected from bugs by enclosing them in light blue plastic bags, so that an area of bananas ready for harvesting looks like an outdoor dry cleaner's rack. Driving through banana plantations in the cool, humid mountain areas, visitors from northern cities are surprised by the heavy, stifling smell of moist corn husks instead of the aroma usually associated with an eating banana.

Because they mature fairly quickly, can be harvested through the year, require little care, and can be grown profitably on small plots of ground (one acre will support about 1,400 banana plants), bananas are an ideal smallholder crop. They were the economic salvation of freed slaves in Jamaica, where bananas started to become an important cash crop in the early 1870s. Banana production on a large scale was begun in the Windward Islands in 1954.

Roseau Valley (top, right) once grew sugar. Now it is covered with bananas right to the head of the valley, which curves around back of the hills at the right. Off the left of the top picture is the *shoreline of Roseau Valley* (bottom, right) where the pier from which bags of sugar used to be lightered to freighters off shore now lies abandoned.

From the heights behind Morne Fortune, are the
harbor and capital of *Castries* (above) just before sunset.
At the center, the town comes down to the water at
the right angle made by the eastern and northern
wharves, which can berth all but the largest ocean-
going ships. On the far shore is Vigie (Lookout) Hill.

Beyond the low hill on the far side of the harbor,
from Vigie Hill northwards, are four miles of beautiful
Caribbean shore along Vigie Beach and Choc Beach.
This area was the site of Le Carnenage, the island's first
settlement and capital. In 1768, the capital was moved
inside the harbor to Castries, which had been settled
as early as 1650–51.

Its sheltered, deep harbor has long made Castries
important to shipping and St. Lucia. Damaged or
destroyed by fire in 1796, 1813, 1927, 1948, and 1951,
Castries has always been rebuilt. After the 1948 fire,
it was replanned and today Castries is a trim little town
of wide streets lined with attractive buildings.

Girls in Creole costume of the "doudou" style.

Spiked French cannon on Morne Fortuné.

On the sunny island of St. Lucia have grown both this smiling girl and her armload of beauty.

Castries Harbor: bottom left, from Vigie Lighthouse; top, at sunset; above, marina.

Come on a quick excursion along the Caribbean coast of St. Lucia.

(Center, right) *Going south from Castries, you'll pass the fishing nets drying on the beach at Anse-la-Raye.*

(Top, left) *South of Soufrière, you pass over the stream on the east side of Choiseul, center of the island's handicrafts.*

(Opposite, top) *Midway across the south coast, a broad beach loafs around the shore of Laborie Bay.*

(Top, right) *At the southern tip of St. Lucia is the beach of Vieux Fort, where fishing pirogues show their ancestry of Carib canoes.*

(Below) *Go north from Castries, and offshore you'll see mile-long Pigeon Island.*

(Opposite, left) *On the dry land north of Gros Islet, manchineel trees grow along the shore, providing welcome shade. It is not wise to stand under them during rain, though, for their orange leaves (opposite, right) have an effect like poison ivy, and even water falling from them can cause painful irritation.*

Tucked in behind a curving entrance and a protective sand bar, *Marigot Bay* (opposite) is deep enough to harbor large yachts. During the rare storm, its waters remain calm, its beaches alluring.

Even on the drive back to Castries at the end of a day already full of pleasure, a turn in the road can treat you to a view of *the Caribbean* (above) from the sunset side of the mountain.

BARBADOS

"Civilized" is the word for Barbados. You see it in the trim, orderly countryside of "little England". It runs like a theme through this precise, articulate island society that has developed along its own line, without interruption, from its earliest days.

The island's first European visitor was its last non-English one. He was a Portuguese captain, who, noting the bearded fig trees near the shore, named the island Los Barbudos and sailed away. Lying 100 miles to the windward of the rest of the Lesser Antilles, Barbados was never in any real danger of invasion. It has remained English from their first settlement in 1627.

For the first 25 years most of the settlers were poor men who paid five years of indenture for small plots of land on which they could grow tobacco. After the usable land was under cultivation, there was no incentive to attract free men, and the government began shipping prisoners while the planters began buying slaves. The Africans nicknamed their white masters "Bim", used today for any resident of Barbados. The more conventional "Barbadian", when pronounced by island residents, comes out something like "Bahr BAY-jdn". This is probably the origin of the shorter "Bajan" (BAY jen), used as both a noun and an adjective.

Bajan and Bim are also the names of publications. Founded in 1942, *Bim* is a literary magazine that continues to be a voice for island writers examining and defining a distinctively West Indian identity.

It was almost inevitable that Barbados should take the lead in this search for identity. Barbados produces a growing number of university graduates. Its population has the highest proportion of secondary school graduates in the islands. Its literacy rate of 98 per cent is one of the highest in the world.

This last achievement is particularly impressive in an area with one of the heaviest population densities in the world, about 1,500 persons per square mile.

Among these are men who've made the island's fishing industry the most important in the West Indies. The *fishermen on Oistens Bay* (right) is casting his net for sprat. Best known sea food of Barbados, though, is the flying fish, brought in to Trent Bay between November and June. Split open, it's about the size of a sole, and whether fried, baked, or broiled it is delicious.

Chamberlain Bridge (above) spans the Careenage at the heart of downtown Bridgetown, the island's capital. The present structure dates from 1898. The town apparently derives its name from the original Indian bridge on this site.

Built of coral rock in 1874, the legislative building, in the background, is the meeting place of the oldest elective legislative body in the Caribbean.

This and the international terminal at Seawell Airport have helped Barbados step up its tourism, although visitors are hardly new to the island. Its climate is so monotonously healthy that it has long been called the "sanitarium of the Caribbean".

An earlier visitor was 19-year-old George Washington, in the autumn of 1751, with his elder half-brother Lawrence, who was seeking relief from consumption. About ten years before, Lawrence had served with colonial troops under Admiral Vernon in the British attack on Cartagena. So great was Lawrence's admiration for Vernon that after he inherited the family home of Epsewasson, he renamed it Mount Vernon.

The admiral's name is associated with another, more racy, institution. Because he frequently wore a weatherbeaten cloak of grosgrain, Vernon was affectionately nicknamed "Old Grog". To help protect them against scurvy, the admiral ordered his men to drink a daily tot of rum and water. His popularity soared and the drink was named, in his honor, "grog".

To return to the "sanitarium" aspects of Barbados, the island's beaches lie in several areas, each with its own personality. North of Bridgetown glitters the

"platinum coast" of luxury hotels and private homes. Barbadians themselves holiday on the wind-swept Atlantic coast. Offering a bit of both, the reef-fringed southeast coast is not as vigorous as the Atlantic, but not as placid as the Caribbean.

Between Bridgetown and Hastings is the Garrison area. Just off the main road is the *public beach along the southern curve of Carlisle Bay* (above), with the Aquatic Club pier and the Royal Barbados Yacht Club premises.

At the end of this curb is Needham's Point. Its old lighthouse has been incorporated into the 14-acre *Barbados Hilton* (right) whose design echoes and incorporates some of the architecture of Fort Charles, which once occupied this site.

Downtown Barbados swings around the statue of *Lord Nelson* (below, right) in Trafalgar Square. This statue was erected in 1813, 27 years before the one in London. It was once surrounded by a green park, now paved and claimed by taxis.

Harbor police wear the uniform of Nelson's tars— bell-bottomed trousers, white middies, and straw boaters—as they cruise out into Carlisle Bay from the *Careenage* where a *fishing crewman* (center, far right) passes the time of day.

Beyond the *donkey cart* is the entrance to Bridgetown's main street and shopping center, Broad Street. From it, narrow little streets scamper off between *18th century buildings* (opposite, center left).

Two blocks back from the Careenage, parallel to Broad Street, *Chapel Street* (opposite, top right) snakes its way eastward into Swan Street, where East Indian shops offer a riot of merchandise and noise, especially on Saturday morning.

Back at the open center of Bridgetown, *young girls in school uniforms* (opposite, bottom right) parade safely toward Chamberlain Bridge. On the other side of the street, *older girls cross Trafalgar Square* (above) toward the legislative building.

The ghosts of gaiety long past are all that remain of the hospitality of *Farley Hill* (left), 800 feet above the sea in the hills of northern Barbados. Built in 1818, this Georgian plantation house had a magnificent drawing room and a spacious dining room, here before you. A broad staircase of solid mahogany swept up to second floor galleries from which tall bedrooms opened out on to cool balconies, where only the sky shows now.

Stately cabbage palms lined the entrance drive when Farley Hill was host to the Duke of Edinburgh in 1861 and later to the Princes Albert Victor and George in 1879-80; the latter was one day to reign as George V.

Barbados did not suffer from absentee landlords. Unlike Spanish and French colonists, English planters preferred to live on their country estates. They built their homes solidly of hand-hewn coral blocks and native cabinet makers copied the designs of Sheraton and Hepplewhite; plate and china were purchased in England. They planted their grounds with the care Englishmen still lavish on their gardens. For recreation they hunted and fished.

When there were guests, they entertained lavishly. At the table they were epic trenchermen; in place of port they drank Madeira, which was so popular that it was exempted from trade restrictions. Madeira was the base of *Sanagree*, a cooling drink still popular in Barbados.

The age that was so golden for the planters passed by completely the survivors of early white settlers who had been elbowed off their small tobacco plantings by the growing strength of sugar. They retreated to the rocky, eroded hills of the Scotland district that rumbles down to the *coast north of Bathsheba* (below).

From a luncheon pavilion on the grounds of Farley Hill you can see miles down the *east coast of Barbados* (above). The rocky Scotland district falls off to the left, down to the coast shown on the previous page. The hills on the right rise gradually to the island's highest point, Mount Hillaby (1,115 feet). Down the center of the picture the land undulates southward under cane to Ragged Point Lighthouse in the distance.

Barbados is one of the most intensively cultivated areas in the Caribbean, as it has been since the 1660s, when most of the usable land had been cleared and put to work. This posed a number of rather special problems when the slaves were freed in 1834.

Agitation for the end of slavery was an outgrowth of the evangelical movement that swept England in the second half of the 18th century. William Wilberforce supplied abolition forces with the leadership and organizing ability that aroused popular opinion against slavery. The decisive blow was delivered by the businessmen who were creating the industrial revolution that brightened the banks and darkened the cities of Britain.

The hoards of people who were filling the industrial cities had to be fed cheaply; protective tariffs kept the price of West Indian sugar high. The industrial products of Britain had to be sold on a world market with free trade; protective tariffs for West Indian sugar were an excuse for other nations to prohibit the free trade of British goods. The abolition forces raised public opinion against slavery because it

was an un-Christian crime; businessmen put pressure on Parliament to abolish slavery because it was an economic hindrance. In 1833-34 Parliament abolished slavery in any land directly under British control.

With most of the land on their island already privately owned and under cultivation, freed slaves on Barbados had little choice but to return to the plantations to work for wages. To provide as many jobs as possible, instead of increasing the yield per man, planters concentrated on increasing the yield per acre through improved cane breeding and more modern production methods.

First things to go were the wind- or oxen-powered grinders, such as the *abandoned sugar mill* (top, right) at the eastern foot of Farley Hill. These were replaced by steam-driven mills with more modern equipment, including heavier rollers. These new mills could squeeze more cane faster, they could extract more juice from the cane, and they could crush heavier, tougher cane than the planters had been growing.

Not content with getting more juice from each stalk of existing cane, they planted the new Bourbon variety. It produced more juice and was more resistant to wind and disease. Through constant controlled experimental breeding, planters have continued to improve the quality of their cane. Today the fields of Barbados grow varieties as thick as this *sugar cane carried by a girl* (bottom, right) on the road near Malvern.

Sugar cane is grown from cuttings of mature cane, planted in November. The cane takes about 15 to 18 months to mature, so crop time takes place from mid-January to June of the following year.

Using the cutlass, the yard-long, wide-bladed knife the Spanish call a machete, *field workers cut sugar cane* (top, left). Separated from the rest of the plants, the *harvested cane is loaded into trucks* (center, left). The hard, fibrous sugar cane is actually about 84 per cent juice and must be rushed to the mill within 36 to 48 hours of being cut, or the juice will drip out or ferment in the stalk.

This simple fact makes sugar both a crop and a product. The two could not be separated. A man who wanted to grow sugar had to have enough money to build mills nearby. Once the mill was built, there had to be enough land planted with sugar to justify the cost of operating the mill. Before long, fewer men each owned more land and the agriculture of many small islands were surrendered to the monoculture of sugar.

A *loaded truck carries cane to the mill* (bottom, left) through the village of Chimborazo. To the right are chattel houses, private dwellings seen all over Barbados. They are two-room houses so simply constructed that they can be dismantled by the owner, piled on a barrow, and moved to a new site when the need— or opportunity—arises.

At the sugar factory, the cane is passed between massive rollers. Cleared of physical impurities, the juice is boiled at successively lower temperatures into a thick syrup. This is boiled under pressure in a huge vacuum pan to produce sugar crystals. The sticky crystals are transferred to centrifugals, large drums with perforated meshed sides, that operate something like a spin dryer. They whirl at about 1,200 revolutions a minute, driving the wet molasses out through the sides, leaving only the dry sugar.

The sugar is usually bagged for shipment. In Barbados, though, it is now taken to the block-long bulk storage plant in the deep-water harbor area, from which it is loaded by conveyor belt into the holds of freighters.

(Right) *Animal Flower Cave far up on the North Point. Centuries of the Atlantic's raging have clawed out three grottos which can be entered at low tide.*

ST. VINCENT

James Bond chose only the best for his personal use. For Bond, and for himself, the late Ian Fleming insisted on short sleeve shirts made, always, of sea island cotton. It has an especially long fiber that produces a strong, smooth cloth. One of the finest varieties in the world is grown in St. Vincent. After the *yellow sea island cotton blossom* (above) falls, the green bulb at its base grows a tuft of the luxurious cotton.

In decreasing quantities, alas, sea island cotton is grown on the drier southern lowlands of the island. St. Vincent's 18 mile length has a mountain ridge running down its center. On the steeper, leeward side grow the bananas and ground provisions that spread down to and around the southern lowlands. On the windward, Atlantic side, the slopes are gentler, producing a rolling landscape with some of the best agricultural soil on the island. This land used to be covered by arrowroot, when St. Vincent grew 90 per cent of the world's supply of that valuable starch. Now, even arrowroot is being replaced by the ubiquitous bananas, which have become the island's main export crop.

In the southern part of St. Vincent the valleys are wide and the eroded hills are fairly low. They rise in height as they go north through Morne Garu (3,523 feet) to their peak of 4,048 feet atop Soufrière, about 3 miles from the northern end of the island. St. Vincent's 133 square miles are almost as mountainous as Dominica. Like that island, St. Vincent has a fairly heavy rainfall, 80 to 150 inches a year, so that it is a richly fertile island.

Although only 5 per cent of the island's land has a slope of 5° or less, over 30,000 acres are under permanent cultivation. Most of the crops are grown along the coastal area and on slopes up to 1,000 feet through the skillful use of contour planting and terracing. About two-thirds of the island's farmland is worked by independent small landowners who have benefited from the government's land-settlement projects. St. Vincent was a leader in the development of independent smallholdings, owing in part, to its comparatively short history of plantation slavery.

Its mountainous terrain made St. Vincent a natural stronghold for the embattled Caribs, who kept both the English and the French off for over a century. The few who did land had to negotiate treaties with the Caribs. The only outsiders who landed safely were some shipwrecked slaves in the 17th century. They mingled with the Caribs to produce a group known, in time, as the Black Caribs. These fought the French, then joined the French to fight the English. The final uprising, known as the Brigand's War, occurred in 1795 when the French and Black Caribs almost wiped out the English, driving the survivors into a stronghold around the southeast port of Kingstown. In June of 1796 English reinforcements arrived, threw the French off the island, and shipped 5,000 of the more troublesome Black Caribs to Honduras. The remaining Caribs were settled in the northeast area, on what was then some of the most fertile land in the island.

Their troubles were not over. In 1812 Soufrière erupted, covering much of their land and a good many of the people. About a century later, two days before the eruption of Mont Pelée on Martinique, Soufrière erupted again, killing 2,000, many of them Caribs. Soufrière has been quiet since; today a freshwater lake fills much of its crater, 2,000 feet below the rim.

After the island became English, sugar was introduced, and the slave population rose to 23,000 at the time of their emancipation. The freed slaves became smallholders, so indentured laborers were brought in: about 2,000 Portuguese in the 1840s, and East Indians, beginning in 1861. When sugar declined in importance, it was replaced by arrowroot, which had been brought to the island by the Caribs.

Of the islands that had once been occupied by the French, today St. Vincent is the most English. Cricket is an accepted mania and Protestant churches—mainly Anglican and Methodist—predominate. The boys are playing cricket in *Kingstown's Victoria Park* (right) with St. George's Cathedral (Anglican) at the left and the Presbytery of St. Mary's Church (Catholic) at the right.

St. Mary's Presbytery never fails to cause comment, most visitors assuming that it dates back to Spanish—or possibly Moorish—times, although neither Spaniards nor Moors were ever on St. Vincent. It was, in fact, built in the early 1930s by Benedictine monks from Port of Spain, Trinidad, under the direction of the Belgian priest Dom Carlos Verbeke. The good father had a retentive memory and an unbridled imagination. Looking rather like something from a Royal Ballet production of *Sleeping Beauty*, St. Mary's Presbytery has an architectural style that is eclectic, to say the least. Built to take full advantage of the trade winds, it is a comfortable building according to its residents, who are Scarborough Fathers from an order outside Toronto; all of St. Vincent's Catholic priests are from Canada.

From 600 feet up among the ruins of Fort Charlotte, you can see St. Vincent's capital, *Kingstown* (above), curving around to Cane Garden across the bay.

Beyond the distant low hills leading down to Cane Garden is Arnos Vale, containing St. Vincent's airport. About $1\frac{1}{2}$ miles along the coast beyond Cane Garden is *Young's Island* (opposite, bottom left), with the Aquatic Club on the shore to the left.

Coming back along the waterfront on Bay Street, you pass the new deep-water wharf, out in the water near the center of the picture, and the *men beaching a sailing canoe* (opposite, center left). As you turn inland, you pass the *garden yard of St. Mary's* (opposite, top left) and catch a late afternoon glimpse of a downtown *Kingstown street* (left) parallel to Bay Street, with Sion Hill rising in the distance.

Off to the left of the picture above, less than a mile from the waterfront, is *Botanic Garden* (3 pictures, far right). Established in 1765, it is the oldest botanical garden in the Western Hemisphere. It was to this garden that, on his *second* voyage, Captain William Bligh brought over 530 plants from Tahiti, including the *breadfruit* (center). This melon-sized fruit with the bland, white pulp caused trouble for Bligh on his first voyage.

Built in 1915, the *Memorial Pavilion* (top) contains a pond in which water hyacinth grow, while locust lilies (quicksilver) grow in the small ponds around it. Royal palms tower regally at the right and cabbage palms as tall as 150 feet stretch beyond the pavilion. On either side of the foreground are the green-and-white variegated hibiscus. In the bottom picture is the spacious fan of a *traveler's palm*, with ropey, red chenille, or cat's tail, plants in front of it.

St. Vincent once supplied as much as 98 per cent of the world's arrowroot, a starch that is valuable in baby foods because it is so easily digested. Although bananas have become the main cash crop, the island still produces large quantities of arrowroot on the fertile, stream-laced hills on its eastern side.

Harvesting is usually done from October through to May, starting from the bottom of the hill and working back and forth to the top. This *woman harvesting arrowroot* (top) near Argyle, in southeast St. Vincent, has pulled up the plant, which can grow to 4 or 5 feet, and snapped off the root. She cuts a small piece from the root and immediately plants it for harvesting in about a year while the main part is tossed onto one of the many collection piles across the fields.

These are gathered by donkey carts and carried to one of four or five remaining plants such as this *arrowroot mill at Biabou* (left).

Fresh from the fields, the roots are dumped into the trough, where water carries them down to the large, revolving drum under the shed in the foreground. Running water washes them clean as they slowly tumble through the drum to the other hold where revolving paddles remove the outside growth.

There they are put through the mill, literally, three times after which the waste pulp is drawn off to be used for animal feed. The milky white liquid remaining is run off into long concrete pools where the pure, white arrowroot gradually sinks to the bottom. The bulk of the water is run off the top. Much of the remaining water is patiently "sponged" out by cloths, until the still moist pulp is firm enough to be removed to the drying sheds.

Here the large chunks are crumbled into lumps and spread on wide trays to dry for 8 to 10 days. When it is dry, the arrowroot is gently raked through the wire screens of the trays, like flour being sifted by a cook. The fine white powder falls to a wide wood table beneath the trays from which it is scooped into bags for shipping.

121

Leaving Kingstown for a quick jaunt to Mesopotamia Valley, you go eastward across the airport runway. (This is no joke: the road—an excellent one—crosses the runway about two-fifths of the distance from its mountain end. It may do much to explain why Vincentians are among the most alert and attentive drivers in the Lesser Antilles.) On the other side of the hills are the *terraced hillsides with banana plants in the foreground* (top, left). Bananas, bananas, and more bananas cover the floor and sides of *Mesopotamia Valley* (top, far right). Mesopotamia is a crossroads village in the valley, which is often listed as Marriaqua Valley.

From Mesopotamia Village you head directly eastwards through *Yambou Pass* (bottom, left) towards the Atlantic coast. Go up as far as Bridgetown and turn around for this view south along the *black sand beaches of the Atlantic Coast* (top, right), where a black rock church stands on the promontory between Grant's Bay and Biabou Bay beyond.

Along the shore of Buccament Bay is Cane Grove Plantation where you'll see *young banana plants being sprayed* (bottom, right).

The last view of St. Vincent is from the same location as our first general view: among the ruins of Fort Charlotte, above Kingstown. Stroll over to the other side of the fort and look northwest, over *Ottley Hall* (bottom, far right) in the valley below, past Lowmans and Camden Park Bays to the open Caribbean.

THE GRENADINES

The get-away-from-it-all spot of the Caribbean, there are over a hundred islands in the Grenadines, with a total area of about 35 square miles. Obviously, some of them are little more than perky outcrops on which you'd be hardput to keep your knees dry, even at low tide. The biggest is only 13 square miles.

The Grenadines ride puckishly along the top of a submerged volcanic ridge for 50 miles south, between St. Vincent and Grenada. Most of

124

them are uninhabited, while those that are inhabited support families who've been fishing for generations. From March through the summer they go out in small boats after whales. The few permanent white settlers have found *the* place to get away from it all.

There are facilities on a few of the islands for guests who like the idea of having nothing to do but swim, snorkel, fish, loaf, and enjoy themselves.

GRENADA

With the lovely inconsistency typical of the Lesser Antilles, Grenada is pronounced "Gre NAY da". It is also called "the Spice Island", which is both poetic and accurate. Grenada is the world's largest producer of *nutmeg* (above) and the network of mace that grows around it.

Nutmeg and cocoa occupy almost the entire mountainous interior. Nutmeg trees grow at the heads of valleys and along steep slopes from just below the forest line to about the 1,000-foot level, where they merge with cocoa trees that grow the rest of the way down. Bananas fill the wet valleys and coconut palms stride along to the shore. Aside from enough grown to make rum, sugar cane hardly counts at all. This was not always true.

After emancipation, planters encouraged Negroes to plant cocoa trees on small sections of plantation land by allowing them to plant the rest of the section in food crops for themselves. When the cocoa trees began to bear, the planters bought the trees for cash, which the Negroes then used to buy clear title to their own land on which they planted more food and cocoa trees, only this time *they* sold the cocoa.

As a result of that early enterprise, about 80 per cent of Grenada's agricultural land is presently owned and worked by independent smallholders. The more immediate result was that cocoa became the island's chief cash crop for 50 years or more until the 1920s, when cocoa was stricken by both witches'-broom disease and low prices. By that time, nutmeg was ready to take over.

Nutmeg has a number of peculiarities that are worth mentioning. It takes about 4 to 6 years before the trees "declare" by putting out blossoms. Only then can the planters tell which are the female trees, the ones that will bear the nutmegs. It takes the trees about 15 to 20 years to reach their peak of production of about 5,000 nuts per tree annually. The ripe nuts are gathered from the ground. The delicate red netting around each nut is removed carefully, because it brings a higher price if it is unbroken. After it is sun-dried to a rich yellow it is mace, a spice that brings a higher price per pound than the nutmeg around which it grows.

The nutmegs are then dried, the shells removed, and the meat of the nut is bagged for shipment. The meat is recovered by groups of energetic women using small hammers to crack the hard shells, usually on a concrete floor. If you close your eyes, the racket sounds like a flamenco troupe going out of its mind.

Grenada has a lot more than spicy nuts to recommend it. It's a toss-up as to whether Grenada or St. Lucia is the most consistently beautiful island in the chain. In its capital, St. George's, Grenada certainly has the most beautiful harbor in the Antilles. It is also the southern headquarters for sailing through the Lesser Antilles by craft such as this *yacht off Grande Anse Beach* (right).

The two-mile stretch of Grande Anse is the queen of the island's beaches. Grenada also offers you your back-to-back choice of a black sand beach on the Atlantic or a white sand beach on the Caribbean along the shores of Pointe Saline. Or, you can join so many of the Grenadians who prefer the palm-shaded sands of Levera Beach on the island's northeastern shore. Whatever your hopeful heart has been looking for, chances are you can find it on Grenada.

The sunset *guns of Fort St. George* (bottom, far right) guarded the harbor entrance when the French built this fort in 1705-1710. Now used as police headquarters, its battlements are a sightseer's delight, from which you see *St. George's in the late afternoon* (top, right).

Most of St. George's curves around the Carenage and used to be called "Carenage town". Off to the left of the picture is "Bay Town", separated from the main part of St. George's by the ridge on which are the Anglican, Presbyterian, and Catholic Churches. Under the ridge, Sendall Tunnel joins the two towns.

The Carenage, at the right, is a deep harbor that was once the interior of a volcano crater, whose outer rim has been eroded by the sea. Schooners tie up at the

seawall, across the street from the waterfront warehouses. Just off the right of the picture is a deep-water pier used by freighters. Beyond that is the Lagoon used by yachts.

Over and beyond them, on the hills at the right are the remains of *Fort Frederick* (above), 800 feet above St. George's, towards which the boys are pointing. The buildings in the background once joined those just below the crest, until Hurricane Janet cut a swath through them in 1955. On the other side of this plateau, *boys huddle over a cannon* (bottom, left) that covered the eastern approaches to St. George's. From its gunport you can see Mount St. Catherine, at 2,756 feet Grenada's highest point.

Getting carnival down on paper is about as likely a possibility as using a hurricane for a domestic air-conditioning unit—and just about as frantic and frustrating. Most of the islands celebrate carnival at the same time. In *some* respects, smaller carnivals are more fun because you can usually stay in the center of things . . . providing your strength holds out. On the left are some bright flashes from the small but lively *Carnival in Grenada.*

Each carnival has a theme song or marching song that has become a favorite from among the pre-carnival calypso contests. Calypsodians are singer-composers with a tradition that goes back to the chantwelle of colonial days. Their songs, or calypsos, are what might have happened if a combination scandal sheet and medical textbook had been written by Gilbert and Sullivan. Their essence is wit and their edge is satire. Grass roots calypso, from which the art renews its strength, is so laced with innuendo based on local reference that it's foolish for an outsider to try to explain it. Enjoy the night club calypsos and let it go at that.

West Indian carnival apparently started through French colonial influence in the islands. Along with parties and masked balls there were torchlight processions in blackface called *canboulay* (probably from the French *cannes brulees:* burnt cane). After emancipation, *canboulay* became carnival and a lot more vivacious, with the occasional merrymaker winding up in the morgue.

Carnival isn't any quieter now, but it's much better organized. The week after one carnival, preparations are begun for next year's event. Carnival usually begins, officially on Lundi Gras, Monday, at six o'clock in the morning with *jouve* (probably from *jour ouvert:* daybreak) and continues on through to midnight of Tuesday, Mardi Gras.

On Ash Wednesday the survivors, some of whom may be in fairly rocky shape, still go faithfully to church, whether in Port of Spain, St. George's, or in the country northeast of St. George's, to the *Catholic Church near Vendome* (top, right). Vacationers can then surrender themselves to the balm of beaches. Prime choice among these is the bright, soft sand of *Grande Anse Beach* (bottom, right).

Sunset in the tropics is quick, with only fifteen or twenty minutes between the scarlet and mauve glow of light and total darkness under a star-flecked sky. There is little gradation here, on these alluring Antilles. The contrasts are sharp.

The air is clear and the lights are bright, the shadows are deep and seething with smouldering colors. In the light the colors are intense, too intense for northern eyes. Martinique forced Gauguin to abandon the subtleties of Impressionism; even in Tahiti he had to evolve his own language. No painter can transcribe the raw color of the tropics the way they are.

We think of them as year-round islands in the sun. Our year has four seasons; their year has two: dry and wet.

The blindingly blue sky always has some clouds and there are occasional showers, but from January to June the islands are usually sunny and progressively drier. Cane is harvested and the bared fields slowly parch to yellows and browns. Stream beds dry to ravines and vines and shrubs shrink closer to the earth's last moisture. The winter's riot of flowers gently fades to softer colors as summer approaches.

Then the rains begin, in June or July. They continue until December, falling most heavily in August or November, depending on the island. They fall heavily, they fall steadily, and sometimes you think they're never going to stop.

Dirt again becomes earth, rich and pungent. Barren gullies fill to flooding with roaring torrents. Fusillades of drops pop like pistol shots off the flopping banana leaves, and the shooting cane swells with juice. Fields that had puffed up dust when you walked across them a few months ago now squish under foot. Then the rains slowly withdraw, leaving behind them the richest Christmas gifts of all.

Sodden fields seem to shake themselves dry like pups after a bath. Ripe and fat, they gleam with a hundred greens under the burnishing sun. Over the fields and among the trees reawakened flowers burst into bright flurries of reds and yellows, oranges and purples.

And over all is the clean, sweet brush of the trade winds against your cheek. Even these refreshing winds suffer from a misconception that, like so many nuisances in these islands, goes back to the 18th century. It was during that time that the "trade" part of the winds was taken to mean "commerce"; they were the winds that brought the trading ships. This was true, but it was not why they were called "trade" winds.

Begetters of romance—and money—the trade winds of the Caribbean blow constantly toward the equator from about the thirtieth parallels, north and south. The turning of the earth deflects them so that they come at the islands more or less from the northeast. They can be counted on always to blow "trade", that is in the same direction, following the same track, or treading the same path. It was from the Middle English *trede* or *tread* that *trade* was applied as early as the 14th century to winds that could be relied upon to tread the same path.

In a way, it's a more appropriate meaning for the name of these winds that bring life-saving fresh water to the islands, for much of the social life of the island is lived out of doors, along the path of the road.

Houses are built close to the roads, so that they won't miss anything; also, of course, so as not to waste scarce land that can be used for kitchen gardens. Along the roads, especially in the late afternoon, you'll pass young girls of seven or eight, or their mothers, carrying home on their heads buckets of water from the tap that supplies each settlement with pure water. On rocks and bushes around the house, you'll see the family laundry draped out to dry in the sun, especially on Sunday afternoons.

Sunday is the great cleanup day. After church men sit on boxes by the roadside, getting their hair cut; women gather to gossip while doing the family wash in stream beds; and, in her open-air bathing lounge, one Sunday morning was this *young woman shampooing her hair in a mountain stream* (bottom, right).

The stream gurgled down from the pool at the foot of *Annandale Falls* (top, right), a forty- to fifty-foot drop with lianas stringing down towards it and giant elephant ear plants flopping up the rock wall beyond it.

This is about 3½ miles northeast of St. George's. Go a little bit farther in this direction, along the road that cuts across the island to the airport, and you'll pass *Grand Etang* (next page, top) a freshwater lake inside a volcano crater. About 1,800 feet above sea level, the lake has a surface area of 36 acres, although it appears smaller. The grass around its edges has roots firmly on the land from where it grows as far as 30 to 40 feet out across the water.

If you leave Grenada on a weekend, you will see one or the other of two events. On the east coast is the island's second largest town, where you can see the *Saturday Market at Grenville* (bottom, left) and the *fish market out on the pier* (right).

If you leave a day later, you'll pass by the *Sunday morning wash in Paradise* (above), a village half a mile south of the airport.

TOBAGO

Tobago is the vacation island for the residents of Trinidad, its sister island about 20 miles to the southwest. It's difficult to keep a good thing secret, though, and more North Americans are finding Tobago every winter.

Tobago has been politically linked with Trinidad since 1889, after having been seized at one time or another by the English, French, Spanish, Dutch, Swedes, and the occasional buccaneer.

Fishermen on Great Courland Bay (above) had trailed their net out in a large horseshoe. Pulling evenly at both ends, they are now hauling in bonito. The net will

often yield such strays as the *crab* at the right. Offshore, *pelicans* (left) do their own fishing from a boat piled high with a net ready to be used later.

Great Courland, Store, and Mt. Irvine Bays, along with Buccoo Reef, have made the flat southwestern end of Tobago a prime vacation resort area. A low range of hills stretches for 18 miles along the northeastern end of Tobago's 26-mile length. On these are grown the cocoa that is the island's main cash crop. Coconut palms take up more area than cocoa, but their copra produces a smaller income.

"... I am persuaded that there is no island in America that can afford us more ample Subjects to contemplate the Bounty and Goodness of our Great Creator in, than this Tobago ...", wrote Captain John Poyntz in 1683, in what must be one of the earliest pieces of Caribbean tourist promotion. And the poor captain didn't have the added pleasure of seeing the young lady strutting along the shore of *Pigeon Point Beach* (left).

This beach is in front of the Pigeon Point Aquatic Club and it's ... well, it's as though all of the resources of Hollywood in its heyday had combined every cliché about a tropical island beach into one ultimate example: a wide stretch of clean sand, coconut palms whose swaying fronds cast oases of shade, the beguiling whisper of the trade wind, shores along water of unbelievable clearness, and, of course, a beautiful, laughing girl with long black hair. (Her hair, alas, is gathered up for swimming in this picture; it flows unchecked in the picture on the cover.)

The water to the right is sheltered by Buccoo Reef, a treasure house for snorkeling. Beginners will find hours of fascination; even non-swimmers can explore it by wading. Be careful of the sun, though. It's strong and it's reflected by the water; the combination can burn the unwary very quickly. With suitable precautions, you can enjoy yourself thoroughly without any risk of ending the day the color of *frangipani* (below).

Lingering for a while to look at the beach from the pavilion pier over *Buccoo Reef* (top, left), we pause for a few more precious minutes before setting off across the island, past *blooming gardens* (lower left), to the capital of Scarborough.

Up here, 425 feet above the sea, an *old cannon on Fort George* (above) still guards an island that history has passed by.

TRINIDAD

Trinidad is a whirl of color, a mix-up of races, a thrust of democratic independence. Geographically an off-shoot of the South American continent, it is as British as cricket and Christmas pantomimes, as African as the rhythm of steel bands, as modern as its huge oil industry, as timeless as the rich Moslem ceremonial of *Hosein*, and as marvellous as the wonder of The Pitch Lake. It is the land of the Calypso Kings, of carnival, of open-air markets, of beautiful beaches with swaying palms. It is at once the most West Indian of islands and the least typical.

Though it is grouped with the Lesser Antilles, it is not one of them, for it is an extension of a South American mountain range; the geology of its sister island of Tobago, however, is similar to that of the Windward and Leeward Islands. Trinidad was a stagnant Spanish colony for 150 years, its culture has been strongly influenced by French settlement, and it has come to maturity under British rule. Much of its population has descended from African slaves, but fully a third of this West Indian nation's people are defiantly East Indian, descendants of indentured laborers; Chinese, Portuguese, and Syrians are represented in significant numbers, too. This island that is strongly Roman Catholic also contains one of the largest concentrations of Hindu and Moslem faiths in the Western Hemisphere.

It is easily the most cosmopolitan society in the Caribbean.

The islands of Trinidad and Tobago were first seen by white men during Columbus' third voyage in 1498. Trinidad was named by Columbus for the Holy Trinity; Tobago, thought to be uninhabited, gets its name from the word for "pipe" or "tobacco".

Trinidad consists of 1,864 square miles, crossed by three east-west mountain ranges. A fifty-mile barrier across the northern end rises abruptly from the water to heights of more than 3,000 feet, then slopes gently southward. The central range has eroded to little more than a highland area, while the southern range rises as high as 997 feet in the Trinity Hills at the southeast corner of the island. From this southeast point, the Atlantic coast of Trinidad undulates northward beside Mayaro, Cocos, and Matura Bays. Along much of this is the Cocal, a mile-and-a-half wide belt of coconut palms that reaches to the shore along many miles of beautiful deserted beaches such as that beside *Manzanilla Bay* (left).

Over on the other side, at the northern end of the island's west coast, along the sheltered waters of the Gulf of Paria, lies Port of Spain, Trinidad's capital since 1783, whose name is one of the few reminders of Spain's least successful attempt to colonize.

After a couple of unsuccessful attempts, the Spanish got a colony going in 1584 on the present site of St. Joseph's, only to see it destroyed 11 years later by Sir Walter Raleigh, who also paused to caulk his ships at The Pitch Lake.

Dutch, French, and even the restless Caribs, harassed the Spaniards until by 1692 there were only 22 of them left on Trinidad. Even disease took a hand, wiping out the cocoa trees the Spanish settlers depended on, so that by 1740 they were able to attend mass only once a year in clothes borrowed from one another.

Then, in 1780, a resident of Grenada began urging Madrid to open Trinidad to immigration, an idea that is still popular in Grenada. Eventually, the Spanish government agreed, providing the new settlers were Roman Catholic, and soon new arrivals began pouring in—chiefly French who were fleeing revolutionists at home, rebellious slaves in Haiti, or invading British forces in the Lesser Antilles. They brought coffee, cocoa, cane, and cotton with them and began import-ing slaves. Soon the population had reached 18,000, including 10,000 Negroes, many of whom were free men.

The last of the Spanish governors, Don Jose Marie Chacon, began to build forts and develop the newly established town of Port of Spain. But war broke out between Britain and Spain, and a blockade by the British fleet forced him to surrender. The island was formally ceded to Britain in 1797. The British con-tinued to govern through the Spanish system of centralized control which, while it deprived the colonists of local representative government, also freed the colored population from legal harassment by the planter oligarchy. By 1810, Trinidad's population had grown to 30,000, of whom one-fifth were free colored people. When all the Negroes were freed by law in 1834, they took up the unoccupied interior of the island, where they began smallholdings of their own.

Freeing the slaves caused a labor shortage in Trinidad as elsewhere. Immigration under a bounty system was tried, a system under which ship captains were paid for every laborer they landed. Immigrants came under this system from Madeira, the Azores, France, Germany, the United States, and other islands in the West Indies, but still they were not enough. In 1845 the first indentured laborers arrived from India, a system that continued until as recently as 1917 and has contributed much to the make-up of the modern community in Trinidad.

Of any event since emancipation, the Second World War had probably the greatest effect on Trinidad. The Americans established bases to guard the oil refineries, bolstering the island's economy and inspiring—if that's the word—the calypso *Rum and Coca-Cola*. Most importantly, the American "invasion" quickened Trinidad's contacts with the outside world, a trend that has been further speeded by the post-war jet age. This has not only brought more visitors to Trinidad, but also it has enabled Trinidadians to travel widely. Before the war, travel was usually limited to students, musicians, intellectuals, and cricket players (categories which are not mutually exclusive).

Cricket. It is a passion in Trinidad. Children play cricket on hillsides, using the stiff bases of palm fronds for bats. Schoolboys play it on side streets with borrowed equipment, and proper businessmen devote their weekends to it. Two such groups, clad in the standard, immaculate white, are gathered for a *Sunday afternoon cricket match on a field south of St. Augustine* (below). Any list of the world's best cricketers will almost certainly include Trinidadians.

Trinidad's political development has been long and agonizing. Tobago, which came under the rule of the Dutch, French, and English a number of times before finally becoming British in 1803, was joined politically to Trinidad in 1889 after the failure of its single-crop sugar economy. By this time Trinidad was being governed by its own legislature. In 1845 Spanish law was repealed *in toto* but it was not until 1925—after 123 years of British rule—that Trinidad finally got a form of representation in its government, and even then voting regulations were so strict that they disenfranchised all but 6 per cent of the population.

Since then, things have moved rapidly. In 1946 the first elections based on adult suffrage were held. In 1950 a new legislative council consisted of 18 elected members and only 6 nominated members. In 1956 party politics were introduced and in a new constitution that year the appointed members were denied any further voice in policy-making. Full internal self-government was achieved in 1961 and Trinidad became an independent nation on August 31, 1962. Parliament meets in the Red House and The Prime Minister has his office in Whitehall.

Carnival, of course, is pre-eminent, taking place on the two days prior to Ash Wednesday. Today it reflects its two hundred years of development, with huge historical bands and masqueraders by the thousands representing clowns, Indians, and devils and the artistic, fancy sailor bands. Carnival means many things: exquisite costumes taking a year and more to make, dancing and revelry, and fantastic designs worked in metal. Carnival also conjures up two uniquely Trinidadian art forms—the calypso and the steel band. During the pre-Carnival season, calypso rhythms throb throughout the island as the calypsonians vie with one another at "tents", seeking the title of "Calypso King" for the year. And everywhere are the steel bands, which have evolved in Trinidad from a variety of historic ways of making music since the days of slavery when drums were banned and men resorted to Tamboo Bamboo, beating their rhythms on lengths of bamboo held over their shoulders. Today, the steel band is a folk-art form admired throughout the world.

Trinidad is a microcosm of much of the world we know, flavored with a hefty dash of West Indian all-spice.

Planters who employed indentured laborers from India got more than they bargained for. For the Indians brought with them not only strong backs to work in the fields; they also brought with them, and retained intact, their language, their culture, their religion, their families, and their ages-old will to survive and to achieve.

Many of them sell produce at the *Eastern Market* (far right) in Port of Spain. The young woman is holding a dachine plant from which she is cutting the leaves to be used, with okra, crabs, and seasoning, in the thick and delicious *callaloo* soup.

Indians brought with them both the Hindu and Mohammedan religions. Largely from Agra Province, the Mohammedans always included some teachers in their number to continue their teachings in the new land, where they built mosques as soon as they could after their arrival. A latter-day successor to the improvised plantation structures is the Jama Masjid, or *Jama Mosque* (bottom, right), in downtown Port of Spain.

Many of the Indians worked on a plantation just west of Port of Spain. That land is now St. James, a residential area owned by descendants of the original laborers. It is the location of the Hindu temple containing the gold figure of *Lord Krishna* (top, right).

With their religion and their language came their women, so that Indian life continued uninterrupted, centering around the family and the community. This solidarity gave them added strength for survival, but tended to keep them apart from the changing society of Trinidad. Since the war, more Indians have been moving into the mainstream of Trinidad life. Astute businessmen and prosperous landowners, they are also to be found in large numbers among the professions.

For an outsider, one happy by-product of this change is the easier availability of East Indian food. For, in addition to its other attractions, Port of Spain is a diner's delight. East Indian, West Indian, French, Italian, Chinese, Portuguese, sea food, land food—Port of Spain's got it! There isn't another place in the Lesser Antilles that can rival Port of Spain for the variety and excellence of the meals available.

(Top) *Inter-island schooners at Queen's Wharf in Port of Spain.*

(Lower left) *Government House, the Governor-General's residence, completed in 1875.*

Whitehall, built in 1905 and now the Office of the Prime Minister of Trinidad and Tobago.

(Top) *At the foot of Maracas Falls, members of the Spiritualist Baptist Church prepare for baptism.*

Older type houses of Port of Spain.

(Lower left) *Monastery of the Ancient Order of St. Benedict, founded in 1912, designated an abbey in 1947.*

The Pitch Lake (above) a 114-acre puddle of asphalt about 285 feet deep, is the world's largest source of natural asphalt. Hot and bare, its surface is firm enough to enable men with pickaxes to come out and dig chunks from it.

Cut sugar cane is hauled by *rubber-tired horse carts* (top, right). Molasses resulting from sugar refining is used to make more than a million gallons of rum a year, about half consumed in Trinidad. Much rum is used in the manufacture of Angostura Bitters, first blended in 1824 as a harmless stimulant by Dr. J. G. B. Siegert in the town of Angostura, Venezuela. Popularity forced Dr. Siegert to make his bitters commercially by 1830 and in 1875 the company moved to Trinidad. Today, four Trinidadians are the only men in the world who know its secret formula and just what goes on inside the *vats and casks of Angostura bitters* in the Siegert Company plant.

(Above) *Mangrove trees wade stealthily across the humid gloom of Coroni Swamp, where oysters grow on trees, crabs walk branches, and birds dine on shrimp.*

(Left) *Wheeling above a cluster of mangroves, egrets come in to nest.*

(Above) *Scarlet Ibis flutter in to rest at sunset.*

(Right) *Egrets nesting in mangrove trees.*

(Overleaf) *Scarlet Ibis wing in from nearby marshes.*

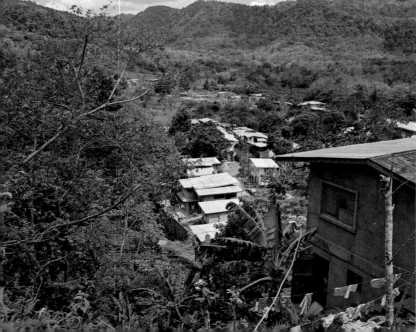

Hemmed in on the south, Port of Spain's growing population has been moving into new settlements in the northern range, such as that in *Diego Martin Valley* (bottom, far left).

From the mountain heights above this valley tumbles *Sylvansintra Falls* (sometimes referred to as Blue Basin Falls), shown on the cover. Its cool mountain water meanders downhill, pausing in shady pools such as the one at the left.

In this area of Diego Martin, Maraval, and Santa Cruz Valleys are the main plantings of *grapefruit* (bottom, left), and *coffee* (top, right), and the experimental station for *cocoa* (center and bottom, right).

Citrus fruits first became important in the 1930s. There are about 16,000 acres of citrus trees, the majority of them grapefruit. Citrus fruits are the third major agricultural export of the island, after sugar and cocoa.

Cocoa needs shelter from excessive sun and wind. Coffee trees provide some of this, but in Trinidad much of the shade is cast by immortelle trees. In the early spring these flare into vivid red umbrellas over the cocoa groves that cover much of central Trinidad and the northern mountain valleys.

Cocoa trees grow as high as 15 to 30 feet. As a general rule, they don't begin to bear until their fifth year, the yield increasing gradually to its maximum in their twelfth year. They may continue bearing profitably until they're a hundred.

Cocoa pods grow at random from branches and trunk, on stalks about one inch long. They are removed with a cutlass and piled in heaps, where the pods are opened and the seeds removed. (Eight baskets of pods will yield one basket of seeds.)

At this stage, the cocoa seeds, or beans, are embedded in a sticky white goo. To remove this pulp and bring out the beans' flavor, they are packed on trays, covered with banana leaves, and left to "sweat", or ferment, for 4 to 8 days. The heat generated by the melting and evaporation of the white membrane slowly roasts the beans. After this, they are spread out in shallow trays to dry in the sun.

Near the end of the drying process, the beans are "danced". Barefoot laborers shuffle through them, laughing and sometimes clapping and singing. While it's fun to watch and fun to do, it has the practical purpose of removing the dried pulp from the beans and polishing them to a smooth, shiny surface.

Sad to say, the "dancing" of cocoa, like the trampling of grapes for wine, is slowly disappearing, being replaced by mechanical polishing done by tumbling the beans in a drum. After polishing, the cocoa beans are hand-sorted for size and quality, and bagged for shipment. Cocoa is sold by the pound, although the usual unit of sale is the fanega—100 pounds.

(Top, left) *Scenic drive along the North Coast Road.*

(Bottom, left) *LaVache Bay, with Maravaca Island in the background.*

(Bottom, right) *Port of Spain's weekend resort, Maracas Bay.*

From the Virgin Islands we have wandered south across these islands in the sun. Now the sun is setting behind the last of our islands, those leading from the *northwest tip of Trinidad* (above) off to the mainland of Venezuela. Our journey is over.

However, another journey is just beginning its most interesting phase. The Lesser Antilles are creating an entirely new people with a distinctive life of their own, built of hope and hard work after almost four hundred years of bitterness and bloodshed. We have tried to show some of this life sparkling through the beauty of its natural surroundings. The beauty of the islands drew us to the Lesser Antilles; the richness and variety of the lives of the people was an unexpected and fascinating discovery.

LEEWARD ISLANDS

ANTIGUA
ST. JOHN'S

GUADELOUPE

POINTE-A-PITRE

DOMINIC

ROSEAU

VIRGIN ISLANDS
ST. THOMAS

CARIBBEAN SEA

N

E

W

S

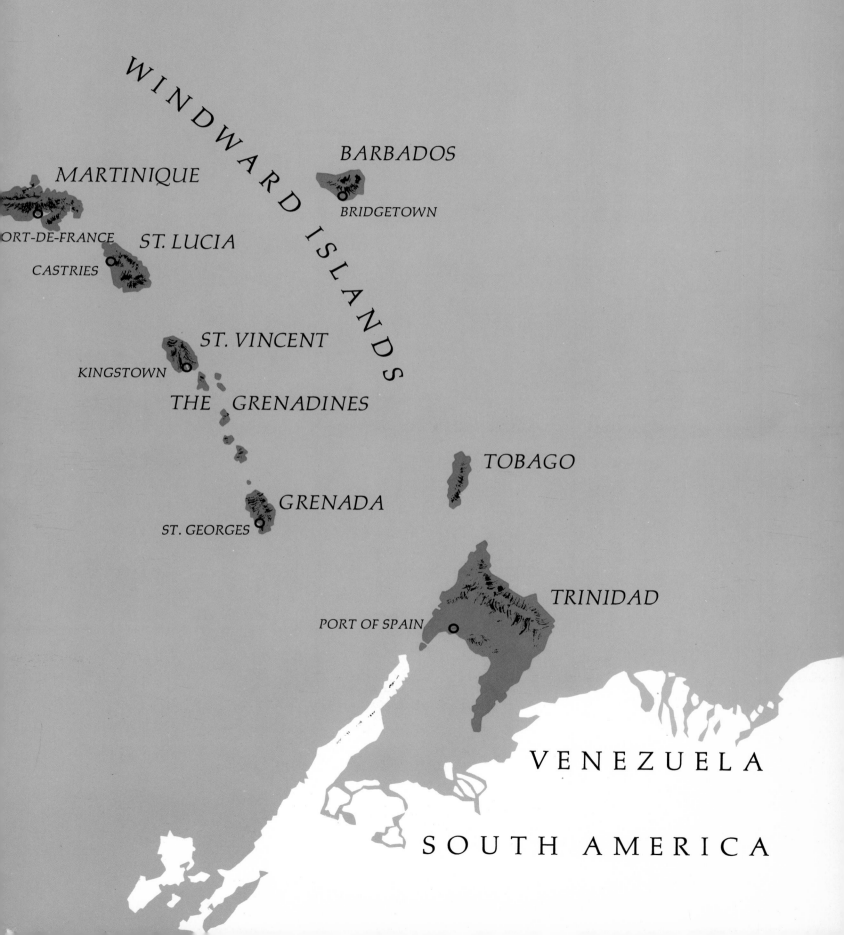

Produced by Quest Travelbooks Ltd.

Color Separations and Assembly
by Graphic Industries Ltd.
and Agency Press Ltd.
Vancouver, Canada

Carnival Scenes (page 130) by Felix Kerr

Typesetting by
Howarth & Smith Monotype,
Toronto, Canada

Film: Ektachrome X (Eastman Kodak)

Camera: Hasselblad